1.95

Craft So Hard To Learn

Conversations with Poets and Novelists
About the Teaching of Writing

Conducted by JOHN GRAHAM
Edited by GEORGE GARRETT

MORROW PAPERBACK EDITIONS

Distributed by
William Morrow & Company, Inc.

New York 1972

Printed in the United States of America.

Graham, John.
    Craft so hard to learn.

    "Morrow paperback editions."
    Interviews originally taped in June, 1970, during the Hollins
Conference in Creative Writing and Cinema for John Graham's
radio program, The scholar's bookshelf.
    1. Creative writing—Study and teaching. 2. Authors, Amer-
ican—Interviews. I. Title.
PN143.G7   808.1′07   72-8798
ISBN 0-688-05017-4

            2   3   4   5   75   74   73

Contents

Preface

This brief collection of interviews on the general subject of the teaching of (thus, also, *learning*) writing comes from a specific time and place, a setting and a situation which were aptly conducive to some very direct talk about the craft and art of creative writing. The writers included in this gathering were all serving as members of the writing staff of the Hollins Conference in Creative Writing and Cinema, which took place from June 15 to June 27, 1970. Some forty-eight poets and novelists served as full-time and part-time staff members for 268 students who came from every state in the nation except Alaska and Hawaii. The period of the Conference was rigorously occupied with an intense schedule of classes, seminars, lectures, and readings, with informal and formal gatherings of all kinds. In this atmosphere it was easy and natural for the writers to talk directly about their problems and concerns, not only as artists, but also as teachers of the craft.

John Graham of the University of Virginia, himself a writer, critic, and a member of the Conference staff, used all the spare moments he could seize, night and day, to tape-record conversations with the writers, critics, editors, and film-makers who were at the Conference, for his educational radio program, "The Scholar's Bookshelf." Together with his skilled announcer and engineer, Rod Collins, he managed to put together 110 programs, each a fifteen-minute, self-contained segment. These programs have been widely broadcast on educational and FM stations.

From transcriptions of those programs I have edited a larger, representative, book-length gathering which will be published by William Morrow and Company. In order to make a book of manageable length and size, and because the conversations included here are of a more specialized nature, I have decided to present the interviews specifically concerned with the *teaching* of writing in a separate publication.

All these writers are teachers, and all of them teach writing as well as literary courses. Some have done so for a good many years. Others, younger, have less experience in the classroom as teachers, though the younger writers most often have *studied with* other writers as undergraduate and graduate students. The result of the range and diversity among the writers—variety in age, educational background, experience, aims and goals—is an equal variety in the ways and means of teaching the craft.

The creative writer, the poet and novelist, is, by now, a familiar figure in academe. There are a few, a handful really, who are simply "in residence" in institutions which can afford that luxury; but there are today very large numbers of working writers, older and young, at the beginning of their writing careers or of well-established reputations, who are also hard-working teachers. They contribute a great deal to the lively study of literature, and, by the same token, their engagement is not restricted, purely and simply to *creative* writing. They are artists who are deeply concerned about reading and writing in all forms, at all levels. Thus, much that they have to say, speaking out of their own experience, is transferable, applicable to different, though analogous situations in learning.

I hope, then, that this brief collection will be of some real value to both teachers and students, that the variety of approaches, even the evident contradictions, will serve to help others in the urgently essential task of teaching writing. I have approached the task of editing these interviews as a work of scholarship, a presentation of *the scholarship of experience*. The conversations are offered in the chronological order of their making. Each comes from a single fifteen-minute tape recording. They have been only slightly edited to facilitate reading in print and, as much as possible, to preserve the sense and qualities of the writer's spoken voice. None has been *revised* or *rearranged* by myself or by the writers who, most generously, have given full permission for their words to appear in this form.

GEORGE P. GARRETT
President, Associated
Writing Programs

JOHN GRAHAM

(Interviewer)

Born 1926 in Washington, D.C. Educated at Georgetown University, Harvard, Johns Hopkins and Georg-August-Universität (Göttingen). Has taught at St. Paul's School, Georgetown University, Marquette University, and Johns Hopkins. Presently Associate Professor of Speech and Drama and Assistant Dean of the College of Arts and Sciences at the University of Virginia.

Books: (anthologies and texts) *Studies in A Farewell to Arms* (1970), *Great American Speeches* 1898–1963 (1970), *Studies in The Second Skin* (1971); (record albums) *Great American Speeches of the Twentieth Century* (Caedmon Records, 1969), *The Wit and Wisdom of Will Rogers* (Caedmon Records, 1970); (juvenile) *A Crowd of Cows* (1969).

1. R. V. CASSILL

Born 1919 in Cedar Falls, Iowa. Educated at the University of Iowa. Was a long time staff member of the Iowa Writers' Workshop. Presently is Professor of English at Brown University. He was founder and long-time president of the Associated Writing Programs.

His books include: (Novels) *Eagle on the Coin* (1950), *Dormitory Women* (1954), *The Left Bank of Desire* (1955), *The Wound of Love* (1956), *Clem Anderson* (1961), *Pretty Leslie* (1963), *The President* (1964), *La Vie Passionnée of Rodney Buckthorne* (1969), *Dr. Cobb's Game* (1970); (short story collections) *Fifteen by Three* (with Herbert Gold and James Hall, 1957), *The Happy Marriage and Other Stories* (1966); (essays) *An Iron Time* (1969); (text and anthology) *Writing Fiction* (1963); (edited) *Intro*, vols. 1–4 (1967–1971).

R. V. CASSILL

(Brown University)

1. It seems to me that the real value and the real essence of any art is to keep moving.

GRAHAM: I think, frankly, Verlin, this is a fantastic idea, the idea of teaching creative writing. It's so easy to throw the obvious question—can it be taught? So maybe we'll slide off that and turn to a book you wrote, a few years back now, called *Writing Fiction*. I've just finished reading it, and, not to be awkward, I am excited about the book. And I'm teased by one of your very early statements in the prefatory note, where you urge the young writer to start really with analytical reading. Now, this bothers me because I know that I'm maybe inclined to over-respect a great writer. So if I were to start with looking at *Moby Dick* or *Anna Karenina* or *The Scarlet Letter*, I'd be frozen. Does this happen with the young writer?

CASSILL: Yes, I think it does. It happens all the time, and the easy antidote to this particular fear of freezing up is to direct the writer to people who are closer to him, people who are more nearly his own contemporaries, and who write in an idiom and about a scene that has more to do with his own experience.

GRAHAM: So he doesn't have to learn too many of the counters then all at once, perhaps?

CASSILL: Well, we begin to read as children, and from there on it's a matter of improving by small steps as our experience increases and our facility with verbal equivalents of experience broadens out. There's no such thing as a perfect reader. And what I urge young writers to do, in urging them to read as writers, is to go on from where they are. A great many people read fiction in a way that might be described as skimming the cream off the bottle of milk. They read quickly through a novel, and they get something valuable from their reading. They get an emotional effect. They get a comprehension of character, but they don't get the whole thing. They get the cream off the bottle, and when they try to make their own bottle of milk, they try to make it out of all cream. They don't know how to build in the substructure that floats these marvelous effects that they've admired so much in someone else's work.

GRAHAM: Would you say that the danger—it's a kind of happy danger—is that they may read a novel as if it were life rather than as if it were life and art?

CASSILL: Well, sometimes they read life badly too. They respond only to the moments of greatest emotional impact. They don't see the connectives between the high moments. They don't see the stuff through which dramatic tensions are built.

GRAHAM: You know, one of the things I find so attractive and impressive, and a little scary, about your book, *Writing Fiction*, is that you start with observation. But by observation you mean a very rich attempt at probing the nature of that sensory experience, don't you?

CASSILL: Again, everybody does as well as he can. And if we start with limited and honest and solid observations, nothing really prevents us from going on a great distance from that, using the same methods. But there is such a thing as faulty observation, as lying to oneself or resting content with comfortable explanations; and I think, even for the writer who'll never be a professional, that the attempt to master the craft of writing can be good for him, good for his soul, not just his mental health, as he learns to face the crannies and the dark spots in his experience, and the dull spots—or the spots that have seemed dull—and sees that they're part of the whole tissue with the excitements.

GRAHAM: I think your whole underlying argument, at least in the early part of the book, is it fair to say, is that it takes courage . . .

CASSILL: Yes.

GRAHAM: . . . to observe?

CASSILL: It's exactly that. And it isn't courage in the simple sense of being able to face a physical danger at all. A great man says, "Courage is not a separate virtue, but it's every virtue at its testing point." And that's the kind of thing I'm talking about—the courage to test one's judgment of what life's about, what one's whole past has been about. And as you noted, in the book I say that most writing begins, when it begins to be honest writing, with a kind of autobiography, a disguised autobiography. But every writer essentially begins the real thing when he turns toward himself.

GRAHAM: Of course, he has to write that whether it's ever published, or whether it's any good or not. He almost has to write that autobiographical first novel to clear the paths for his imagination.

CASSILL: Sure, and autobiography is not as simple and clear-cut a term as we sometimes think. There is, for instance, the example I've very fond of—Hawthorne and *The Scarlet Letter*. He's writing superficially about events that had occurred a couple of centuries or more before the time in which he wrote of them; so it can't be, technically speaking, autobiographical. And yet so much of the passion in the book, so many of the insights, so many of the moral relationships between characters seem to come out of his own life and beyond that seem to be the best revelations we have of the real substance of his inner life, to reveal more about Nathaniel Hawthorne than the things that are technically called biographies. Which is what I think fiction really does at its best for anybody, whatever his level of professional competence.

GRAHAM: One fascinating line—and I don't want to phrase this so it sounds like some cheap justification—one thing in here that you talked about was that the idea of writing—trying to write, let's try that—is in itself a liberal art, that this is the sort of thing, as you said, that may permit a man to face his own soul or discover his soul en route in some way. And I suspect that I had always looked on writing courses as . . . well, maybe vocational in a sense, that you must be planning to become a writer. And yet obviously, with the structure you have suggested here, it's much broader.

CASSILL: This leads back to a favorite idea which is that writing and reading are not neatly separable activities, that we use the same disciplines, the same leaps of the imagination to read well as we do in writing. And again, it's a part of my method as a teacher to keep sending the young writer to this book or that book or another book to see things that are related to his own writing; not just to find models that he can copy, but to find the extensions and dimensions of human experience. And what I do think is that when one increases the scope of his own craft and learns to write better, he also learns to read better. It pays off both ways.

GRAHAM: A little like the argument that the two years of piano lessons are hardly going to prepare you for the concert stage, but you're going to listen to a great pianist much, much better.

CASSILL: There's great truth in that, and in one way or another it tends to be suppressed or ignored. I paint some. I'm an amateur painter and a very good amateur painter, and what I find literally is when I spend an afternoon painting a watercolor, let's say, I may be totally dissatisfied with the picture I've made; but I go out into the evening and I see variations of gray in the buildings standing up against the sky that I wouldn't have been aware of if I hadn't been at work on my own picture just before.

GRAHAM: This is a lovely argument, the whole idea of not doing too well, but sharpening your contact with life through this clumsy experiment. Do your young writers by the time they commit to a course in writing with you at Brown University—do they discourage fast, or are they able to hang in? Or is that maybe one of your major functions, to help to hang in?

CASSILL: *Ee-oo-um* . . . complex question. You're going right to the heart. I think they hang in. The only thing that's disturbing is they get to a certain level of comfort where they know they've accomplished something and are scared to go on, afraid of spoiling what they've already learned how to make.

GRAHAM: Like a first-rate pro who just keeps rewriting his first novel, or his second novel perhaps.

CASSILL: Sure.

GRAHAM: A charge that's often leveled at Hemingway of course, that he didn't take chances.

CASSILL: And it's certainly true of many writers, and I think this is unfortunate for them and for all their readers. I don't think that's what writing or any art is about. It seems to me that the real value and the real essense of any art is to keep moving. I'd much rather see a limited young person making some expansive movements than see an accomplished pro repeating himself. I think there's sickness and bad health for everybody involved in this tendency to stay still with the level of accomplishment.

GRAHAM: If we don't grow as human beings or as artists, we're bound to wither down.

CASSILL: And to wither people around us too. I don't hold much with that.

2. *I don't believe that there can be, except in very rare cases, successful fiction that depends entirely on dialogue.*

GRAHAM: *Writing Fiction* breaks down into a number of sections, Verlin, and I can see the middle one is set up of examples. Would you want to talk with me about your general concept? Why did you break the two sections of theory up with the big chunk of examples?

CASSILL: That was a mere convenience, to put the examples in the middle. Matter of typography rather than conceptual design. On the other hand, the three parts of the book do fit together, and all add up to something that might be called the method that I'm trying to expound. The first section has to do with the mystery of the craft, the finger exercises: the formal arrangements of language of scene and half-scene, of expository passages, narrative passages, and so on. But every writer has to deal with these as a matter of housekeeping or carpentry. That's the shape of the first section. Then the section in the middle is a group of examples of contemporary short stories. And I put them in because I think every writer needs to have a group of stories and a group of novels that he knows very, very well.

GRAHAM: I think you used Matthew Arnold's term someplace in your book of the *touchstones*, so that he can turn to quickly and really know almost every line of the story, so he can find out how another man turned a corner.

CASSILL: That's right. Arnold is speaking of masterpieces, and I'm not claiming these are masterpieces. But they're fine stories, and each of them is a little different in its approach. Some of them are told in the first person; some in the third; some depend very heavily upon scene, and others are much more composed of narrative; tone is important in one and so on. So they do form a small kit of examples that the writer needs. Then, in the last section of the book, I've spelled out some of the fundamental critical concepts that a writer needs in dealing with the general outlines of his own work, the big shapes, the meaning of his own work, and in examining, analyzing, isolating elements in the things he reads. I do emphasize that the reading and his skill in reading are a very important part of learning his craft. And I've dealt in the last part of the book with such things as plot, character, theme, and the unity of a story, tried to show by example and definition what we mean by unity. After all, life goes along without any real seams; so a writer has to ask, "Where do I begin? How do I know this is the beginning? How do I know when I've finished my story?" So he needs some working critical concepts to help him sharpen his notion of that kind of thing. That accounts for the design of the book as a whole.

GRAHAM: I'm inclined to feel that the placement of those examples is key, if I may intrude, because I think with so many books of craft, if you will, it's so easy to spin theories. I've been taught the idea of unity and tone ever since I started grammar school, and yet it was always conceptual, really. I don't think it was until very, very late in college that I started to get any sense of what this was. You know, the very end of the book is a tease for me. You list, as you say, a handful of novels that could really help the person trying to move from the short story into the novel form; and you list *The Great Gatsby* by Fitzgerald, *By Love Possessed* by Cozzens, *The Wild Palms* by Faulkner, *The Day of the Locust* by Nathaniel West, and then *Parktilden Village* (which I don't know) by George P. Elliot, as well as Chekhov's *The Duel*. Now your book was published in 1963, was it not?

CASSILL: Yes.

GRAHAM: I was wondering is there anything you'd kind of like to add to that list at this point?

CASSILL: Again, these examples weren't chosen because they were great masterpieces. They were chosen for the sake of variety in technique and approach and theme and tone. And probably if I were asked by a student to suggest another handful of novels, I might include some others: some that occurred to me almost at random, though they're books I admire very much, are . . . for example, a quite strange book, a sort of grotesque American book, called *The Lime Twig* by John Hawkes.

GRAHAM: I'm delighted! I'm a real fan of John Hawkes and *The Lime Twig*. That's his most accessible book in a way.

CASSILL: Right, and the book in his whole production which is most satisfactory to me; because it bounces right on the line between a sort of obscure and mystic surrealism and a realistic story. There's a dimension beyond realism in it, but I don't get lost in a fog of other-worldly processions.

GRAHAM: Certainly with *The Cannibal* and *Second Skin* he's manipulating time so much it might be very difficult to follow.

CASSILL: Very difficult, and something is lost in the difficulty, some of the tension and suspense and the feeling of unity, I think, goes. Well, other examples here are a novel by Brian Moore, who's an Irish-American writer, essentially, American novelist, called *Answer from Limbo.* . . .

GRAHAM: I don't know that one.

CASSILL: It's a beautifully constructed book about a writer, and I think it might be valuable to a writer because of its subject matter as well as because it's so marvelously done. And then, the novel *Revolutionary Road* by Richard Yates, who's here with us at the Conference, is both a first-rate novel and an example of a nearly perfect piece of craftsmanship. It was published, I think, in 1961 and was very well received and admired because of the hard, fully rounded concreteness of the development of the story, of the plot line, the setting, the groups of characters who are set up to play their parts at various points along the way as the story develops.

GRAHAM: I'm interested in the Brian Moore, if we may go back to another one of his—*I Am Mary Dunne.* I know of your concern with that narrative voice, how valid that voice. Are you familiar with that book?

CASSILL: I read it this past year, and it's . . . he's a good writer. But I don't think this is one of his solidest books by any means.

GRAHAM: I've got problems with it, and I hope to discuss the novel with him later on in the Conference. Well, how do you feel poetry functions for the man who sees himself essentially as a fiction writer?

CASSILL: Oh, I think it's absolutely of the first importance for the writer of fiction to learn how to read poetry.

GRAHAM: Is this for language or for general form?

CASSILL: For both. Poems as we know them are usually shorter, but there are certain formal elements that stand out more clearly in poetry than they usually do in fiction, but which have to be in a work of fiction if it's to be successful. And to sharpen your reading ability by devoted reading of poetry pays off just as well as reading fiction. I think we ought to read drama too. We are to find the story methods, the narrative methods in film.

GRAHAM: Your deep commitment to Chekhov's plays, which is revealed in your book, *Writing Fiction,* will indicate immediately how important the formal structures of drama are.

CASSILL: Indeed, yes! And I think I say somewhere in the book that *The Duel,* which was given to the world as a novelette or short novel, is really Chekhov's greatest play. He's put it together just as he put his best plays together. He's massed his characters in separate partisan groups and brought them together in a sort of initial conflict, allowed them to move apart, and brought them back into a more deeply knotted conflict, and carried them along individually and as groups to a resolution, very much as he would do it on the stage and as it needs to be done within the limitations of the stage.

GRAHAM: Within your own work you use a great deal, do you not, of dialogue?

CASSILL: Well, yes and no. I don't believe that there can be, except in very rare cases, successful fiction that depends entirely on dialogue.

GRAHAM: Who am I thinking of, Ivy Compton Burnett?

CASSILL: Yes.

GRAHAM: And Henry Green.

CASSILL: Right. And these are tricks. They're not essentially working in the mainstream of fiction, however fine they may be as tricks or as exceptions. But I keep saying to my students—don't imagine that you're writing a play. The theater has certain advantages that you don't have, and you have to make full use of your advantages. The great advantage of fiction is, you do have a mix. You can talk in general terms; you can foreshorten time in narrative passages. You can describe with some concreteness and some emotion the quality of a passing year. That can't be done on the stage.

GRAHAM: I remember the fantastic section in *To the Lighthouse* where Virginia Woolf—a whole twenty-page section in there where she has the years wrapped up. It's all foreshortened.

CASSILL: All fiction takes advantage of this ability to change pace, to move in close and slow things down, and to dramatize, use dialogue, give us the feel of the moment and the way it's developing to a crisis, and then to slide away from that and tell us what the consequences were, over the years, and on a variety of characters. And the writer who doesn't feel ready to take full advantage of this flexibility, I think, is handicapping himself very drastically.

2. WILLIAM PEDEN

Born 1913 in New York City. Educated at the University of Virginia. Has taught at Virginia and Maryland. Presently is Professor of English at the University of Missouri. Served as Director of the University of Missouri Press 1958–1962.

Books: (short stories) *Night in Funland* (1968); (novel) *Twilight at Monticello* (1972); (historical studies and editions) *Some Aspects of Jefferson Bibliography* (with Adrienne Koch, 1942), *Life and Selected Writings of Thomas Jefferson* (with Adrienne Koch, 1944), *Selected Writings of John and John Quincy Adams* (1946), *Increase Mather—Testimony Against Profane Customs* (1953), *Thomas Jefferson—Notes on the State of Virginia* (1954); (texts and anthologies) *Twenty-nine Stories* (1960), *The American Short Story* (1964), *Short Fiction: Shape and Substance* (1971), *New Writing in South Carolina* (with George Garrett, 1971); (juvenile) *Golden Shore: Great Short Stories Selected for Young Readers* (1967).

WILLIAM PEDEN

(University of Missouri)

1. No matter how good the instructor or the leader of the group might be, if he tries to force his own ideas or if unconsciously he imposes his own ideas upon his students, I think he's very likely to destroy whatever talent they have.

GRAHAM: Professor Peden is before me right now in the guise of a teacher of writing. I realize, Bill, that you are dealing with a highly self-selective group of students. I mean, the student has surely at least attempted a few poems, a few stories, before he puts himself into your hands or at your feet or whatever he may do. What are his chances, really? Is tenacity "all" in this sort of thing?

PEDEN: Tenacity is part of it. A student has to have some ability to begin with, some native ability. Call it talent.

GRAHAM: He's got to have more than hope, then.

PEDEN: He's got to have more than hope. He has to have more than ambition. He has to have more than the ability to learn. On the other hand, talent alone obviously isn't enough, but without a certain amount of ability, all the hard work in the world isn't going to get him very far.

GRAHAM: I often feel I have a dead ear when I reread things that I have written, much to my discouragement. How do you start off a young student? Do you have a clear-cut developmental pattern that you normally will use or do you work with them pretty much as individuals?

PEDEN: You have to work with them as individuals. Students that I have in my writing seminar at Missouri have a certain amount of training when they get to me; most of them are either advanced undergraduates or graduates who have had a beginning course. They know the basic mechanics; so I have a pretty good and well-weeded out group to begin with. And, within that kind of framework, I guess my basic concept is that I must work with them individually, try not to force my own preferences or prejudices upon them.

GRAHAM: This must, in fact, be very difficult.

PEDEN: It is, in a way. It is. . . .

GRAHAM: If you wish to write realistically, yourself, or if you see satire as the major form, it must be hard to hold back.

PEDEN: It is and this I think is the major weakness of what can be an inherent kind of evil in the "teaching of writing" courses, because I think that no matter how good the instructor or the leader of the group might be, if he tries to force his own ideas or if unconsciously he imposes his own ideas upon his students, I think he's very likely to destroy whatever talent they have. A lot of people whose opinions I respect do this sort of thing, and they don't agree with me. They feel that you should specifically channel kids in one direction or other. I don't agree with that at all. I think that each student is a completely individual case. And, what I think I try to do is to give a certain amount of professional advice. There are certain things you can say about technique. There are certain ways of building a scene or handling dialogue.

GRAHAM: In other words, give them the capacity to exercise some options?

PEDEN: Exactly, yes.

GRAHAM: Do you have everyone in a particular class at least experiment with fantasy, experiment with polemic?

PEDEN: No, I never do that. I have them all do certain basic assignments over a period of time, certain basic exercises in dialogue or in plotting or building a scene or doing description. But, above and beyond that, I try to let them find their own way to a certain degree, or I fall back on Faulkner's comment that the person who's really any good must and will become a writer. Eventually, he finds the way to do it, or is found by his subject matter or found by his ideas.

GRAHAM: It's a little bit the way Dick Wilbur was talking in that wonderful poem where the landscape defines the man.

PEDEN: That's right, and it's hard to explain that sort of thing to someone who is not creatively oriented. It sounds awfully pretentious, to a certain degree.

GRAHAM: Or mystical, maybe?

PEDEN: Mystical, right, and Lord knows, writing is not a mystical matter in most ways. It's a matter of conscious knowledge, conscious effort, assuming, as I said to begin with, that one has a certain amount of talent, of creative ability, to begin with. That's the basic denominator, I think, upon which everything must be based. Above and beyond that, it seems to me, a writer develops the same way a good athlete develops, or a lawyer, or a doctor, or a surgeon.

GRAHAM: He learns the moves and then forgets he's learned them, keeps refining on them—I don't want to say unconsciously—is this fair?

PEDEN: No, I think it's more conscious than that, that you learn certain things, there are certain things you have to do, have to know, just like the warming-up exercises of an athlete or finger exercises for a piano player, or simply learning how to apply pigment if one is a painter. And then, that having done the groundwork, it seems to me, if the person is not just a competent putter-together of words, he begins, eventually, to find the method or the shape that his fiction will take at the same time he finds the subject matter. It's a matter of trial and error, of course, and it takes place over a long period of time with most people.

GRAHAM: They tell me that the real time for courage for the young writer is when he's, oh, about twenty-five, and he looks up and sees that a lot of the people he finished college with are, if not exactly established, are leading "normal" lives, and he still has the orange-crates and the paperbacks smeared all over and no money.

PEDEN: There's not much money, certainly not in poetry or short-story writing.

GRAHAM: I know I've made, as I'd hazard most men have made, these rather abortive attempts at writing. I'm sure I have at least one file drawer filled with potential stuff. But I know one thing that's interfered with me, as an academician, is the reading, the constant reading of first-rate fiction and poetry. I was wondering how you use the corpus of English and American literature—any literature—to help your students and yet not intimidate. I can't imagine myself writing *The Great Gatsby*. A book like that just stops me absolutely dead, making me want to be very good as a writer or no writer at all. Does this happen with your students?

PEDEN: Well, what I try to do, both with my students and in terms of my own writing, is that—particularly to the comparative beginner—everything he reads should be something from which he learns a little technique. I think a writer, particularly a young writer, has to learn to read professionally and critically and analytically.

GRAHAM: You mean this consciousness must be not only in the writing, but in his reading?

PEDEN: He gets to the point that he reads a short story, or a poem the same way an architect reads blueprints, or an athletic coach analyzes plays and film of the opponent's game. Because regardless of how the form changes—and that's one of the interesting things, of course, about the short story, the fact that it is so fluid and so flexible—regardless of how the form changes, there are basic narrative methods which don't really change. That is, there's one way, or maybe a hundred ways, of getting a character out of a room or across a river or across an ocean, and regardless of whether you're writing virtually plotless fiction or traditional stuff, there are certain basic narrative methods that one can use. And in the apprenticeship period, I try to get my own students constantly to be reading, critically and analytically, as I've said, and constantly to be writing.

GRAHAM: They learn, then, by "translating"?

PEDEN: You learn technique, you learn how Hemingway begins a story, if there is a specific kind of Hemingway opening, as opposed to the way Faulkner begins a story, or how does—I'm using only traditional authors—how does Saroyan handle dialogue as opposed to the way, say, Flannery O'Connor handled it. In other words, there's enormous variety, but *within* a relatively stable part of techniques.

GRAHAM: With your emphasis on form, and following a sort of buried lead you gave me earlier, do you encourage, or have you made any use of other art forms? Would you normally encourage your students, let's say, to take a course in the film, or painting, or music?

PEDEN: Yes, particularly, it seems to me, since the whole cinematic history of the last twenty-five years has been enormously influential in changing the shape and dimensions of fiction. And I encourage my students to go to as many movies as possible, or simply watch television scripts.

GRAHAM: Bill, when I was in graduate school, I did everything I could (it was a very traditional program I was in) but I did everything I could to justify every concert I went to and every movie. "This was all part of the art."

PEDEN: That's right, that's right. Painting, too. I think they can learn a good deal from painting.

GRAHAM: The galleries—and I've done a good bit of work on this—the galleries, for instance, for Hemingway. He was always talking about Cézanne, saying that he learned how to get people in a landscape with the landscape "real."

PEDEN: And they learn a good deal about color. A good many young writers are not aware of the fact that, that color is really a narrative method.

GRAHAM: Go ahead. What do you mean?

PEDEN: Well, Dos Passos, for example (who was, parenthetically, first trained as a painter), has a kind of visual approach to fiction, and his stories are full of color, full of physical color.

GRAHAM: Sort of tangerine, watermelon? Does he use lots of color words?

PEDEN: That's right, while another writer will be highly conscious of the sense of smell. And this is something that the comparative beginner knows nothing about. "One thing that's wrong with your stories, there's no smell in them." And they think you're kidding them. It's a minor element, but still part of the whole complex fabric of fiction. And this is something, you see, that they can learn by thinking about and participating in arts other than the written.

GRAHAM: I certainly thought of Keats, with all his use of taste.

PEDEN: All the senses, all the physical senses are in Keats.

2. *If you'll read H. E. Bates, I'll read Hawkes.*

GRAHAM: You're bringing out a book fairly shortly, around the beginning of 1971, on *Short Fiction: Shape and Substance*. I like the subtitle. Would you talk about the book some?

PEDEN: There are two parts, really, to the book. The first is an extended essay, a short book in itself, in which I talk about what I consider the form, the varied forms, of short fiction: the short-short story, the so-called short story proper, and the novella or nouvelle. I have attempted to arrive at a kind of definition of the various genres in the overall term of short fiction.

GRAHAM: How long have you been teaching short fiction now?

PEDEN: For about twenty years.

GRAHAM: And you have *Night in Funland and Other Stories* issued.

PEDEN: Yes, I've been writing short stories.

GRAHAM: That's rather hazardous, isn't it? Taking your own chances as a creative writer while you're teaching?

PEDEN: Very hazardous, yes, but also a lot of fun. The short story has had broad appeal to so many different kinds of writers over so many years because it is a very flexible literary form. It's an extremely varied form. It can be almost anything really. It can be just about what the author wants it to be.

GRAHAM: Why would that be? You're saying it's more flexible than the novel, where you've got so much room to manipulate?

PEDEN: It's more flexible than the novel because it's more strictly contemporary than the novel.

GRAHAM: I'm not sure I understand that.

PEDEN: In certain ways, it's almost like a news story. It's very firmly rooted in reality, whereas the novel, or long prose fiction, for two or three centuries, had nothing to do with day-to-day reality. Fanciful romances. . . .

GRAHAM: No one ever had to go to work, which confused me.

PEDEN: That's right, no connection with reality. Now, the novel and the short story do, and have, shared the fact that they are frequently concerned with day-to-day reality. On the other hand, we have fantasies, we have romances, and we have that sort of thing. Let's put it this way: in one major line of its development, the short story was concerned, not with adventures in a never-never, Faerie-Queene-allegorical kind of area, but with the problems, specific problems, of real people doing real things at a particular time of history and in a particular place. That's true of the novel, too, in one line of its development, but I think maybe perhaps because of its very brevity, the short story tends to be a form subject to change. Actually, as you know, what we call the modern short story is really relatively new—a hundred to a hundred and fifty years, whereas poetry and all tale-telling go back almost to prehistory. The drama and various poetic forms are ancient. The novel and the short story are relative newcomers to the so-called family of literary types.

GRAHAM: I would think, too, that one thing that could encourage the short story would be the development of new techniques of printing and the wide distribution of periodicals.

PEDEN: That's an important historical fact. Unlike any other literary form in the entire course of history, the growth of the short story coincides with the growth of periodicals and newspapers.

GRAHAM: Which must be bound up with the broad-based literacy in Western culture.

PEDEN: Why weren't there short stories in the seventeenth century? For the same reason there weren't television scripts in the seventeenth century. If you don't have television, you don't have television scripts. Until you had periodicals, which presented in short space something for a developing mass audience, you had no short stories. It grew up as the middle class developed in the middle of the eighteenth century. Basically it was originally a queer temporary form with no real claim to literary distinction. It wasn't until the generation of Poe and Hawthorne and, in Russia, people like Gogol and Turgenev around 1830–40, thereabouts, that the short story began to become an art form as well as a means of entertainment or moral instruction or whatever.

GRAHAM: Now, in *Short Fiction: Shape and Substance,* as you described it earlier, you were distinguishing between a "short-short story," a "short story proper," and a "novella." Would you talk about those distinctions a little bit, because I'm someone who has almost lost his skull over the novella as a form, that hundred-page "novel." I think of Thomas Mann, of Flaubert with the *Three Tales*, obviously Henry James.

PEDEN: This is something which I find fascinating. I don't know that people other than specialists will. It would be very simple and very misleading and dishonest to say that a short story differs from a novel, or a novella differs from a novel simply in terms of length. That actually isn't the case. Obviously a short story is shorter than a novella, and a novella is shorter than what we call a novel or a long work of prose fiction. I really think that isn't the actual point of reference. What is the point of reference is not so much length, but it is the whole concept of what the author is trying to do. Let's put it this way: the novella is more complex, or can be more complex than the short story. It can have the emotional complexity and density of a novel, but it doesn't have the broad panoramic sweep of the novel. The short story, at least in one major direction, focuses on and emphasizes a few moments. They may be days or years or simply moments of elapsed time, but it focuses upon a single or related group of incidents involving usually a very small cast of characters. The novel, on the other hand, can have enormous complexity, cover enormous chronological time, great shifts of scene, and that sort of thing. Somewhere between the two lies what Henry James called "the beautiful, blest and shapely novella." At its best—as it is in some of the authors you mentioned, and in a great many others, particularly in the last thirty years—the novella has the complexity, or it can achieve the complexity, of the longer form within confines which are more like the shorter form. But it's a matter not just of length alone. That, I think, is completely the wrong way of going at it . Basically, it's a matter of concept. It can be highly complex, intellectually, emotionally, but it doesn't have the broad succession of incidents that we find in the novel.

GRAHAM: What you're suggesting is that a novella tends toward poetry in its compression?

PEDEN: Not necessarily. I think the short story tends to be somewhat akin to lyric poetry in that it achieves a kind of unity of effect or totality of impression, what Poe called "totality of effect." You can call it "wholeness," or "oneness" or "harmony." Call it what you want, but I think the only thing one can really say is that it is silly and arbitrary to try to make rigid definitions. You can't because there are no hard and fast lines of when a short story is no longer a short story but is a novella.

GRAHAM: It's like trying to distinguish between poetry and prose. There are places where you can't tell.

PEDEN: Exactly. This is something for the literary specialist or the historian. I think it can become extremely dull and actually extremely pretentious. The novella is the most challenging perhaps of all literary forms, and for that reason it has attracted really, the very major talents: Flaubert, Conrad, James.

GRAHAM: I had forgotten Conrad. Go ahead with some of the others. You say that in particular the last thirty . . .

PEDEN: Again without making rigid or arbitrary division I think of a story like William Faulkner's "Barn Burning." It has the depth and density and variety of a novel—incredible story! If there's anything such as greatness in short fiction it is a piece like Faulkner's "Barn Burning." It achieves just about the greatest potential that the form is capable of. Or James Joyce's "The Dead," to go back thirty or forty years. It's relatively brief in terms of pages, although it's much longer than the average short story. But to compare it to *War and Peace* or anything that without argument we would call a novel, it's brief. Yet, within that thing, just as Faulkner does in "Barn Burning," Joyce re-creates the essence of an entire way of life, middle-class Dublin at the turn of the century. Faulkner, incredibly, not only in "Barn Burning" but in half a dozen others, captures a whole way of life of three or four generations—planter aristocracy, redneck, poor white—that sort of thing—a fading aristocratic society which ended long before 1865 in Appomattox, a whole sweep of history, various social classes, and an engrossing story line, all within a matter of about ten thousand words. It's incredible!

GRAHAM: *Short Fiction: Shape and Substance* is, for a significant part of it, a book of theory. But, Bill, if I may be presumptuous, I think quite rightly you've included a group of stories in there, so anyone can take that theory and immediately connect up with the reality of writing. Who are some of the authors, some of the stories, that you felt served your purposes?

PEDEN: I'll preface this by saying that what I've tried to do is select stories which are good in themselves and at the same time suggest or illustrate the extreme diversity and complexity of which the form is capable. And I have, for example, some relatively simple, what I would call "one-incident narrative sketches," like Stephen Crane's "An Episode of War." Which is a very brief vignette, involving a lieutenant during the

War Between the States suddenly being wounded by a sniper's bullet, one episode, one single intense episode. At the other extreme, I have another war piece, which I would call a novella or conceivably a short novel, although I think of it as a novella—William Styron's *The Long March*, which involves the accidental killing of a group of enlisted men during training in North Carolina—an accident of war, like the Stephen Crane. Between those two extremes, the single, intense situation, the Crane story and the much more complex counterpointing of past and present of William Styron's story, which begins with the simple statement of fact that these men have been killed by a misdirected mortar shell. Then Styron goes deeply into the past to trace the events in the lives of the commanding officers and the Captain and Lieutenant which culminated in that catastrophe. . . .

GRAHAM: Where did the catastrophe come from?

PEDEN: That's right.

GRAHAM: The strange pursuit of history and memory that, it seems to me, every artist is involved with.

PEDEN: That's right, and I've tried to include stories which suggest just about every basic narrative method, every attitude, every point of view, to which the form is susceptible. I have among the better-known stories Joyce's "The Dead" and William Faulkner's "Barn Burning," which to me come about as close to perfection in short fiction as one can imagine. If the term "perfection" in a field of the arts has any meaning, I think we'll find that in these two pieces. You know, there are very few things perfect, but these two stories in my opinion come very close to that state.

GRAHAM: Any new writers that you might direct me toward, or writers that I just might not have heard of? I didn't find out about Turgenev until a very few years ago. I thought I was rather widely read, but he was a major discovery for me. Do you have anybody like that tucked away?

PEDEN: I've got some contemporary authors who are not well known. They're not "unknown," but they certainly haven't been accorded the recognition they deserve. One of these is the man whom I consider the leading English fiction writer living today, a man named H.E. Bates. He's simply a very great.

GRAHAM: I've not read him.

PEDEN: He's simply not read in this country. He doesn't even have an

American publisher anymore. And he is one of the literary phenomena of our times.

GRAHAM: What would you suggest I start with in H. E. Bates? Any particular thing of his that you like?

PEDEN: There's a collection of stories of his titled *Colonel Julian* from which I have selected a story called "The Frontier." The collection was published about fifteen years ago, both in England and America, but like most volumes of short stories, it did not sell. It was not read, and it wasn't even very widely reviewed. H. E. Bates is, in my opinion, a real master. He's fairly well received in England. He's a man now in his late sixties who has published about forty or fifty books, and never has published a bad book. I've read about twenty-five. He simply is a great craftsman in the great tradition. Another author, who is about the age of Bates, maybe a bit younger, happens to be a close personal friend of mine. That's Ward Dorrance, who lives in Washington, D. C., and, unlike Bates, he is not at all prolific. He has published two or three books in his lifetime, but in his own way he is a master in the tradition of Flaubert, Conrad, and James, of the highly polished, highly artistic work of craft as well as entertainment. I have a story of his.

GRAHAM: You're depressing me, by the way. I haven't heard of him at all, you see.

PEDEN: That's one reason why I have him in the book; because very few people have heard of him. I have a work of science fiction by a very little-known and quite young English science fiction writer named J. G. Ballard. As you know, science fiction, for the most part, is not what you would call a significant literary form, although it's capable of becoming it.

GRAHAM: There's nothing intrinsic about it that keeps it from significance. C. S. Lewis did some rather wonderful stuff in science fiction.

PEDEN: C. S. Lewis has done fine things, and this young man I think is really quite exciting, and has a real future ahead of him. I have his science fiction story in the book. I have ten or eleven authors like that, who are really good, but have just never been popular.

GRAHAM: You mean in your book I can find some of the people and get the bibliographies of their other works? Do you recommend other stories by them?

PEDEN: Yes. There's a brief biographical sketch of each author and lists of the author's major books in there.

GRAHAM: To go to a novella, have you read John Hawkes's *The Lime Twig?*

PEDEN: No, I haven't. I know John Hawkes's work, but not well enough to discuss.

GRAHAM: I'm so keen on it that it's almost a moral obligation for me to force people to go after Hawkes's fiction.

PEDEN: If you'll read H. E. Bates, I'll read Hawkes.

GRAHAM: All right, fine. Is the novella still a continental form? Are we getting material from France, Italy, Germany, do you know?

PEDEN: I know it's being written in Latin America, which is about the only other literature other than English and American with which I am at all familiar. I think, unquestionably, it's becoming an "in" form again. Even publishers who would not look at the form twenty-five years ago are beginning to. They're having to, because there are some tremendous achievements being done in the form today. We already mentioned Styron. Eudora Welty did a superb novella some years ago, *The Ponder Heart.* I would say from about the time of Eudora Welty's *The Ponder Heart* and Hemingway's *The Old Man and the Sea,* along about the middle of the 1950's, the form began coming back, surprisingly enough. And tremendous things are being done.

GRAHAM: Now, I don't mean to bring in an artificial thing, but can you talk to me a little bit about the problems of publishing? It seems to me when I was a boy, young man, in the thirties and forties, every magazine—and there are many of them that have died—every magazine had a couple of short stories. Books of short stories, it seemed to me, sold then. Why don't they move now? What's happening?

PEDEN: No one seems to know. Actually, publishers don't know, statisticians don't know, literary historians don't know. One thing is fairly certain, though. Television to all intents and purposes killed the mass circulation popular magazine market. No question about that. And that's simply an unmistakable fact.

GRAHAM: Has television also sucked off people who might be short-story writers, but now they're writing scripts?

PEDEN: Unquestionably. An interesting example: H. E. Bates, whom I mentioned earlier, told me that his son, very early in the son's career, wrote a script for television and made a great deal more money on *one* television script than the father had made for ten books over a period of ten years. So the son just stopped writing fiction and wrote television scripts. And, as you said, fewer and fewer publishers, commercial publishers, are publishing volumes of short stories. The university presses are beginning to move into the field.

GRAHAM: Louisiana State University did your collection, *Night in Funland*. Where they felt that there was such a gap, as with publishing poetry, the university presses had to come in and, bluntly, help out.

PEDEN: This is true. The whole publishing picture is changing. The individual publishing firms are disappearing, becoming part of enormous conglomerations, everybody's merged. Within the last six weeks, two major American independent publishers have merged. More and more magazines, the good magazines, are no longer accepting unsolicited material. It's a very dark picture for the young writer.

3. FRED CHAPPELL

Born 1936 in Canton, North Carolina. Educated at Duke University. Since 1962 has been at the University of North Carolina at Greensboro where he is co-director of the Writing Program.

Books: (novels) *It Is Time, Lord* (1963), *The Inkling* (1965), *Dagon* (1968), *The Gaudy Place* (1972); (poetry) *The World Between the Eyes* (1971).

FRED CHAPPELL

(University of North Carolina
at Greensboro)

*I've seen persons come alive to themselves
in writing classes in a way they never have
done before.*

GRAHAM: Fred, I'm confused. I have been talking to many of you men who are first-rate fiction writers and poets and who also teach creative writing. I know you've had lots of cheap shots thrown at you—you know, "Art Can't Be Taught" kind of thing—and I'm not going to do that to you. But, is this a fair question? What are your expectations when you meet with a class? It's a self-selected group. They think they're writers, or they think they want to be writers and presumably they have at least a few poems or stories actually written which seems to justify enrolling in your course. What do you expect to happen, in the four months or a year that you might have them?

CHAPPELL: I guess, to begin with, it is a cheap shot to say that writing can't be taught or art can't be taught. It's a cliché at any rate, but, you know, it's largely true, too.

GRAHAM: That's why I'm nervous about the question.

CHAPPELL: I don't expect generally to get a great short story, a great poem, a great novel, in my writing class. Things that can be taught: you

36

can teach someone how to read someone else's work; you can teach people to read technically for the first time, a Chekhov short story just to appreciate what most people generally just don't see in a short story, the obvious things—how you get a character in and out of a room, what kind of little foibles he has in his voice, what kind of little tics he has that make him this kind of character, rather than another kind.

GRAHAM: In effect this is not dissimilar to the rather old argument that your two years of piano lessons, when you bitterly hated them, in fact permit you to listen to a first-rate concert in a way that I can't possibly do.

CHAPPELL: That's right. You hear Mozart in a different way, just as you hear literature in a different way once you've learned those first things. One thing you can teach, you can teach people how not to write.

GRAHAM: You mean there are certain standard traps that you can keep people away from?

CHAPPELL: There are certain traps, indeed. There are certain things that everyone does when they first write a short story or a novel or whatever that are absolutely wrong.

GRAHAM: Can you tell of some of these that you've come on regularly?

CHAPPELL: This is going to sound a little pedantic, but I can do it. Point of view is often all messed up, completely messed up; age difference— since I deal with young writers—they have no notion what a person five years older than they are thinks.

GRAHAM: They can't make that leap?

CHAPPELL: No perspective. They don't have it, of course, so that, often, the best writing you get from young people is first person: what I did when I did do one thing in my life worth writing about. It's the one thing they remember. And then, of course, the themes are often the same among young writers: growing up, so forth, you know.

GRAHAM: But this is basically healthy for them to turn in on themselves and their own memories, their own experiences. That surely is a place where they can find out where their feet touch ground, isn't it?

CHAPPELL: I've seen persons come alive to themselves in writing classes in a way they never have done before. A writing class can be very painful and embarrassing because most of the young people are talking about the thing that really most interests them. Too often, it's themselves.

But often it's something interesting that they haven't really thought about, or thought about in this objective way you have to.

GRAHAM: We get a certain distance into our minds and souls and then we back out pretty fast because we don't want to examine too far, and I guess the writing makes them keep going, doesn't it?

CHAPPELL: It does in a way. There's one traditional way that you can divide a professional writer, a person who's been writing a long time, from the beginning writer—even a good beginning writer. And it's "good manners." A real professional writer, like Henry James or Wright Morris, would be a good example of this. They have terrifically good manners in their stories; there is this distance that won't embarrass you. But a young writer may just embarrass you so much you want to get up and leave the room or crawl under the table or stick your head out the window. But it's powerful, it's there.

GRAHAM: You mean he strips too raw-handedly?

CHAPPELL: He *doesn't* strip in a way; because he hasn't yet put on any clothes. He hasn't learned that yet. And I'm not saying his writing does get worse when he does learn it. It doesn't; it gets to be another kind of writing. But those first, early, crude productions are often . . . perhaps it's a difference between a really well-made Hollywood film and an early Soviet film, where you have raw power, just power, but it makes that impression. It does it to you in a way that a Sam Goldwyn film sometimes just doesn't do it to you.

GRAHAM: I would think one of your greatest problems, and you've led me toward this, is that with so much ego there as I hand you these five poems that I've really been sweating over, these are not casual, I want you to like them, admire them maybe. How do you handle this situation?

CHAPPELL: Fortunately, it's just not the teacher and the student in a room, it's also the other students. Generally, these days, I find myself—students are so sharp now, they're really brilliant students now—that their "worst" audience, their most critical audience is never me. I find myself in the position of defending a student, but their comrades or confrères just tear them up one side and down the other. I spend most of my time patting them on the head after a class and saying, "Oh, what does he know? He's the same as you."

GRAHAM: Given what you're saying here, with this problem of learning a craft and, concurrently, or before really, trying to learn something about oneself, it must be a matter of your function being to encourage, to encourage them then to have courage.

CHAPPELL: That's right. And of course it's often raw egoism. It's probably raw ego that makes us all write even when we're ninety-nine years old. The student himself knows that there is a difference between his short story and the Chekhov short story we read today as an assignment. He knows there's a difference, he can see it. Matter of fact, sometimes he sees it too sharply, and encouragement is essential. You have to quote things from Chekhov to him that show that Chekhov had to begin, too.

GRAHAM: Do you have students read biographies and letters of writers to give them some sense of what being a writer is? That it's not just *The Duel,* or "The Overcoat" or "The Killers," it's not just the finished product that you and I as readers—and the students as readers—see, but the horrors of writing?

CHAPPELL: I do that. Sometimes I'll even read aloud a story I consider—an early story by, say, Chekhov—that I consider a failure as a story, though it's interesting in other ways. Or I'll read Rimbaud's first, awful, sentimental poem about the lost orphans on Christmas Day to them. Or you can just have a student go read *Titus Andronicus.* What a piece of junk that is and the greatest writer in the world wrote it! But he had to begin.

GRAHAM: I purposefully started to talk with you about this awful business of so many of us wanting to "be" writers rather than to "become" writers. We would love to have our corpus up on the shelf, but we don't quite understand there's a process that has to go on. Do you use, I almost want to say, "teasing techniques" to get people experimenting so that they do, in fact, learn the tools of their trade?

CHAPPELL: Yes, you do, and now more than ever you have to, because I think over the past—perhaps I'm wrong about this—but over the past fifteen years the writing class in college has got to be such a normal thing that now I have a whole class of stories, a whole genre of stories that I can almost say this is "a good writing-class story." Now you have to challenge them a great deal more to do experimental things—the things they used to do when I was in writing class—people would do odd, crazy things. Perhaps they would get called down for it, but now you don't get enough of those. Sometimes you get a story that sounds good in class, that does that thing that a short story does, but unfortunately does it so small that sometimes you can't see it. The students are so sophisticated about the class that they know what kind of story is likely to go, both with their friends and with the professor.

GRAHAM: That's depressing. Everyone learns that approach in any class soon enough. In writing an analysis of Wordsworth's images you know what kind of paper the professor likes, so you start using your rhetoric rather than any real logical art. But I didn't realize that would happen in your creative writing classes, too.

CHAPPELL: You know there are even a lot of creative writing classes in high school now, so they already know the word "symbol" when they get here. It's too bad, in a way.

GRAHAM: That's interesting, because when I was in high school twenty-five years ago, I never heard of a creative writing class in high school, and I know they were very rare in colleges at that time.

CHAPPELL: Exactly, but it's just one of the things. It is one of the ways you do get a student involved in the curriculum and interested in school itself. It's always been good for that even when the writing class failed. I mean there wasn't any writer at all in it, and no hope of ever getting a good writer out. The purpose of the class was to draw a student perhaps into English literature, perhaps into any kind of intellectual endeavor.

GRAHAM: This is interesting, because basically what you're saying here—not basically, but you are coming back to it regularly—that the writing class is not an end in itself by any means; nor is it pre-professional training, so much as it's a chunk of the liberal arts, teaching a person how to observe, how to probe, how to read. And this really is what any of us are doing in a college classroom. I just hadn't thought of it in those terms. Do they continue in writing classes? I mean, does one go on or do you feel that, after a year, if the man can't take his luggage and move, that there's no longer much value in it?

CHAPPELL: A year's not enough time, but there does come a time when you have to wean a young writer from school. This is usually done through the mail after he's moved away, keeps sending you stories. You say, "Well, now's the time to go out and face the hard cold wind—you'd better send your stories out to magazines."

4. RICHARD WILBUR

Born 1921 in New York City. Educated at Amherst and Harvard. Has taught at Wellesley and Harvard. Is now Professor of English at Wesleyan University.

Books: (poetry) *The Beautiful Changes* (1947), *Ceremony* (1950), *Things of This World* (1956), *Poems of Richard Wilbur* (1957), *Advice to a Prophet* (1961), *Walking to Sleep* (1969); (translations) *The Misanthrope* (1955), *Tartuffe* (1963); (other) *A Bestiary* (with Alexander Calder, 1955), *Candide* (with Lillian Hellman, 1957); (juvenile) *Loudmouse* (1968), *Digging for China* (1970).

RICHARD WILBUR

(Wesleyan University)

I think even at very good schools—even amongst very good students nowadays— there's an extraordinary patronizing attitude toward the past, and even Walt Whitman is pretty well ignored unless he's thrust upon the students.

GRAHAM: Mr. Wilbur has agreed to talk for a bit here on the problems—the expectations, Dick?—the joys, the horrors, of teaching creative writing. You have, of course, a preselected audience. I guess anybody who enters your writing course enters with something of a little bundle of poems or "attempts" already before him?

WILBUR: Yes, although I don't look at the bundles in the case of my course at Wesleyan. 1 have a feeling that there are so many reasons for trying to write verse that there's no reason to winnow the class too severely and cut out all those who don't have a professional future. If one did, there'd be scarcely anyone there.

GRAHAM: How much variety do you see in the advantage—just to the student—in a class in writing poetry?

WILBUR: There may be no advantage at all, especially for the student who has a real gift and is driven to write. For someone who's part way there and is of the kind of temperament that requires some pushing, I think it is possible that it'd be some help toward an ultimate professionalism. I think I've pushed a couple of students in the class who are now the authors of a number of published books. Of course, you can't show anybody how to write. He must have the ability. But you can sometimes be one jump ahead of him in discovering the writing he might best do. You can help him economize a little.

GRAHAM: I know I've run into people who have that dreadful problem of being, shall we say, rather good short-short story writers and felt compelled—because the novel's the right thing to do right now—to try the novel when they simply could not handle the larger stretch. So you are suggesting that you can, rather than correct bads, encourage goods, in various directions?

WILBUR: Yes, you can find that someone has a gift for epigram, for instance. Let him know it earlier, a few weeks earlier, than he'd have discovered it for himself, and so justify posing as his teacher.

GRAHAM: With poetry in particular, do you work with types of poems? I know you're particularly interested in form, with your translations from various very particular and set forms. Do you have your students exercise with sonnets or brief epigrammatic poems?

WILBUR: I don't try that because, well, if I did there'd be general rebellion. I wouldn't get away with it. I think in any case I wouldn't want to try it, because I don't want to turn my students into clever executors of formal problems. I want them to start the way any kind of poet starts, with the matter, with the urge, and then find out what aids—what formal aids—might make the urge clearest. About once in a semester I will ask people to go and find some form or other, preferably not too tricky, and write in it. And nowadays, given the universal suspicion of anything artificial, this usually means that I'm asking people to write their first formal poem. Often it is no more difficult than the writing of *haiku* in a pattern of five, seven, and five syllables, or the writing of a quatrain. That's all right by me; because I really wouldn't like to see the results if I required a lot of inexperienced writers to plunge directly into the Petrarchan sonnet.

GRAHAM: I remember John Bullitt many years ago at Harvard gave us the alternative of writing a paper on Pope or an imitation of Pope. A number of us opted for the imitation. We learned a great deal about Pope, and I'm afraid his hair grew very gray in one semester. It was a lesson in the nature of Pope's compression that I don't want to have to learn twice in a lifetime. Do the students—it suddenly struck me when you were talking about form—are students now interested in Whitman, with his "Ginsbergian" approach to things? Do students read Whitman now?

WILBUR: It's amusing to call Whitman Ginsbergian because Ginsberg is so Whitmanian. I think pretty highly of Ginsberg, though, as I always feel bound to say, I think he's a rather flawed talent, flawed by exuberance and by his commitment to a kind of a *guru* sideline. But he is a very genuine continuator of Whitman and continues almost everything there is in him, both form and content. But you were saying, are students interested in Whitman? I think even at very good schools—even amongst very good students nowadays—there's an extraordinary patronizing attitude toward the past, and even Walt Whitman is pretty well ignored unless he's thrust upon the students. I thrust him upon my students in the course I give in American poetry. And I'm always pleased to see their eyes pop open when they see what they regarded as the ideas of Alan Watts are, in fact, over a century old in America and a good deal older elsewhere.

GRAHAM: I had to learn that the hard way, with Emerson-Whitman-Thoreau. In general do you use the technique of stimulation, of having your students read a great deal of poetry? Or is that walking them into the dangerous trap of reading finished, even great poems which might kill their nerve?

WILBUR: I'm not worried about that. I tell them to read all over the lot, in all centuries of English language poetry, and then to read the poetry of other languages if they have any capabilities in other languages. I am aware that it's possible to get daunted by the great, and to find oneself imitating, helplessly, to one's disadvantage. But I try to counter this by suggesting that people cultivate twenty enthusiasms at once, if possible.

GRAHAM: Many a novelist has been ruined by cultivating the one Faulknerian enthusiasm.

WILBUR: Indeed. Indeed that's so, but it's a risk worth running, I think, because if there isn't the succumbing to Yeats or Auden or someone that knows how to write, what will be left is Leonard Cohen and the lyrics of Bob Dylan, you see. And this will not accelerate the development of any student writer, I think. Or any young writer.

GRAHAM: The enormous lust that we have for reading leads us to an enormous amount of junk. And basically you're arguing that if you must read, it had better be around some very strong centers, such as Auden or Yeats.

WILBUR: If one is going to imitate, and one is, it's as well to be oppressed with Dante. Most people who have a real letch to write, I think, are people who have the neither good nor bad habit of reading almost everything. I read all four—well, how many sides are there to a cereal box? About six, I guess. I read what's in the catsup and Worcestershire sauce, and I see no merit in that. It's just a bad habit I have.

GRAHAM: We might work out some arrangement where we could have sonnets printed on the back of cereal boxes. I think we could raise the level of poetry reading considerably. I can remember so clearly, and I'm sure it must have happened to you, the overwhelming shock of Eliot, when I reached college. I couldn't believe that this was the way, this enormously allusive way, the way that you use in some of your poems, of writing poetry. Do students react to this with the enormous sense of continuity, the brotherhood of literature really? Do they use these allusions?

WILBUR: The best students, I think, still respond strongly to Eliot. Almost all students are, as a matter of course, if they're English majors, made to study "Prufrock." Often, it seems to me, by the time they reach me, they've studied it two or three times. And they like that. As for *The Wasteland*, "Ash Wednesday," *Four Quartets*, that's accepted willingly by fewer. And it's forced upon fewer. The generality of young students nowadays seem to me not to be interested in the difficult allusive poetry. They seem mistrustful of its sincerity and they prefer a blurting, posterish kind of poetry, I think.

GRAHAM: Are you getting, in your poetry course now, much of what you might call polemical writing in verse? The sort of manifesto from your students?

WILBUR: Oh, yes, I get a certain amount of that, indeed I get quite a lot of it. Some students fall under the spell of people like Lawrence Ferlinghetti or Denise Levertov, or well, you know, there are a whole lot of poets who in recent times have written in particular against the Vietnam war. Usually they take a while to become discriminating in an aesthetic sense between good protest poems and bad ones. The good ones are actually very few.

5. HENRY TAYLOR

Born 1942 in Loudoun County, Virginia. Educated at the University of Virginia and Hollins College. Has taught at Roanoke College and the University of Utah. Currently Associate Professor of Literature at American University.

Books: (poetry) *The Horse Show at Midnight* (1966), *Breakings* (1971).

HENRY TAYLOR

(American University)

No poet who's any good should ever forget that in some real sense he is playing games.

GRAHAM: It's essentially teaching of poetry that you do, is it not? Or the writing of poetry?

TAYLOR: I teach an introductory course in creative writing for absolute beginners, which involves both fiction and poetry. But there's rarely more in there than introducing freshmen and sophomores to the basic problems that they're liable to confront later on.

GRAHAM: In terms of the long haul, how long—or can it be measured?—can, or should, maybe for his own health, a student be a student of creative writing? I mean, how much can you do for someone—I'm presuming he does have quantity of talent—how much can you do for someone after an introductory course and, say, a seminar?

TAYLOR: Quite a bit, I think. I mean in some sense I'm still a student of creative writing, and there are people that I regard as teachers.

GRAHAM: Suddenly I feel rather stupid. If the growth factor isn't there, you might as well stop writing yourself now.

TAYLOR: Right. However, one thing that you say is worth continuing with. There is a danger that a student can be an official student too long, a hanger-on, a person who can never turn loose of a thesis, for example.

GRAHAM: Of course, I know the analogies with dissertation writers. I would imagine a couple of things happen there. If a man can't find his own pacing, if he can't—well, frankly, if he can't stop writing for particular people, such as a favorite teacher or something like that—trying to please Papa, he hasn't got much chance of growth, does he?

TAYLOR: There's some time you've got to cut loose, but even after you've cut loose from the initial surroundings of a writer's workshop or graduate writing program, you'll always have someone, hopefully, that you'll trust.

GRAHAM: The judgment, the character, the sensibility. Now that we're talking, we're learning right now, for instance. I mean, you and I've known each other for some five years—I read your first book of poetry that came out what—*The Horse Show at Midnight* was 1966, wasn't it?—I read that a couple of times, and our relationship, while not teacher-student by any means, permits learning from each other, I presume. What do you do with the more advanced student? He's self-selected, he's got a sheaf of poems, probably at the beginning of the course.

TAYLOR: I teach two upper-division courses in poetry writing. One is designed more for the student who maybe has not written much in the way of poetry at all, ever, and he comes in and I take him through a quarter of the bitter basics.

GRAHAM: Why might a student who didn't already sort of define himself as poet, why would he take this course?

TAYLOR: All kinds of reasons. People do this: they suddenly decide they're interested in writing poetry. They suddenly run across a poet who turns them on. Or, very rarely, and a happy case, the very good English major who wants to know more about that side of things. He's been taking critical courses all along, and he's developed a set of critical methods which he feels he can improve, broaden, by means of seeing it from the other side, so to speak.

GRAHAM: Step into, in effect, the psychology of the artist. What does one do when one's got two thirds of a poem done. What happens at that horrible juncture really.

TAYLOR: That kind of thing. And most of those students are always a pleasure to have because most of the time they wind up writing better than they ever thought they would. And they have very perceptive and useful things to say to the other students, the ones who always thought of themselves as poets and therefore in some way have not done as well in the other classes. This was my situation at Virginia, if you may recall. I used to cut classes a lot.

GRAHAM: To write poems. This is particularly interesting because you're bringing another facet of the variety of values that derive from a poetry-writing course. Verlin Cassill, for instance, argued very persuasively that it was analogous to the two years of piano: you can never play very well, but you can certainly listen so much better. A quarter with you of trying to make these vowels and consonants and ideas behave themselves is going to make me a better reader.

TAYLOR: Right.

GRAHAM: Do you use— Will you have students, in a sense, "exercise," to follow the piano thing? Do you make them write sonnets, for example?

TAYLOR: Yes, absolutely, I start them out on metrical exercises, work through couplets, four-line stanzas, five-line stanzas of their own invention, sonnets; and then I introduce them to a variety of weird, insane formal games that various poets have played over the years—starting with the more traditional ones, such as ballades, villanelles, sestinas, and the like. And then you move on to acrostics.

GRAHAM: Oh, really? I don't mean to be facetious now, but you sort of play games at certain points?

TAYLOR: Sure. Sure you do. No poet really who's any good should ever forget that in some real sense he is playing games.

GRAHAM: This is certainly reflected in your own poetry, where you have written some desperately serious poems, very disturbing poems, but grouped in with those very serious ones are wisecracks, almost firecrackers under the table. I should imagine some of them have been annoying to people, by the way; we can talk about that perhaps another time. Then, basically you're trying to—by your use of form—you're setting them through an exercise pattern from which then they will walk away?

TAYLOR: Probably, probably. Especially as things stand now. The problem is in the current literary scene. You have a situation where a poet somehow feels obliged to declare rigid loyalty to one way of writing or another, and there are few exceptions to this. Robert Lowell is one. Robert Lowell has said, in fact, "I do not see why I should do this."

GRAHAM: You mean they want to be part of a school? In a traditional sense, maybe?

TAYLOR: You have some who think that rhyme automatically leads to doggerel. At the other end you have someone like J. V. Cunningham, who says, quite flatly, somewhere, "Poetry is the definitive statement, in meter, of something worth saying." And if a poem doesn't have at least meter, it's not for him.

GRAHAM: Could we back up just a little bit? Poets have always, I mean within my experience, been involved with "schools," and finding people that they could work with, compete with, maybe. But it did seem to drop out. Do you want to comment on why you think they need this sort of definition? Is the world too big and different and so much experimentation going on that they want some kind of catalogue slot for themselves?

TAYLOR: I don't think that's as prevalent now as it was, say, in the early part of this century, say between 1909 and 1917, when schools proliferated to the extent that you could start a fake school and get everybody interested in it in a serious way.

GRAHAM: With a manifesto attached.

TAYLOR: Right. But now, though there are schools, you have, for example, the poets who got started about the same time as Ginsberg and Kerouac and that crowd, and the New York poets, Frank O'Hara, Michael Benedikt—so on—John Ashbery—all of whom I think—except O'Hara, who is dead—worked for the magazine *Art News.*

GRAHAM: Do you see this as perhaps a useful device? I don't mean to sound quite so artificial, but for a poet, a young emerging poet, to find a group that gives him some sense of direction, at least for a while?

TAYLOR: I think it's risky. Any bunch of poets that gets to be thought of as a bunch of poets, is in trouble in a way because the reading public—such as it is—is going to begin to lump them together. And people will say things like, "You know O'Hara, Benedikt, Ashbery, and that crowd." And then the distinctions between their poems, the difference between Benedikt and Ashbery, for example, will become blurred.

GRAHAM: I would think that the real danger would be that the man would not find his own voice, whatever the readers may think. He may someway speak in a collective, an editorial "we," with all the dreary flatness of an editorial. May I ask this, Henry? In your experience in reading students' poems, are you getting much polemical thrust? Are you getting manifestos in verse, given the activism on campuses now?

TAYLOR: Some. It's an odd thing, but it seems to me that in America—for reasons that aren't clear to me, and I've thought about it a lot—writing a political poem, a poem about Vietnam or a poem about the assassination of President Kennedy, something of the kind, seems to require from the poet a kind of attitudinizing or posturing that is not required of a poet say—I think immediately of a young Finnish poet named Pentti Saarikoski, who lives 120 miles from Leningrad. He has a poem called "120 Miles from Leningrad." For him, political realities are human realities. For Americans, somehow, political realities don't seem to be human realities.

6. MICHAEL MEWSHAW

Born 1943 in Washington, D.C. Educated at the University of Maryland and the University of Virginia. Has taught at Virginia and the University of Massachusetts. Presently traveling in Europe and Africa. Plans to resume teaching during 1973.

Books: (novels) *Man in Motion* (1970) and *Waking Slow* (1971).

MICHAEL MEWSHAW

(formerly University of Massachusetts)

I think too many young writers spend a
great deal of their time trying to express
some deep, dark, vague, amorphous
reaction to their own experience of youth,
and I personally think it would be more
beneficial to focus on, perhaps a personal
experience, but a smaller experience, one
that they can come to grips with in a
conscious fashion, and shape.

GRAHAM: Michael Mewshaw's career as a novelist is just beginning with the birth of *Man in Motion*. I've been talking with a great many of the staff here at the Hollins Conference and one of the things we've been working over is how do you teach creative writing; what are your expectations; what are the frustrations, the problems, maybe even some of the techniques. Now, could we kind of switch that a little bit and go at you with the first novel? Can you talk a little bit about learning to write from your point of view? You did take some creative writing courses formally? Who did you work with?

MEWSHAW: Well, at first, as an undergraduate, I was at the University of Maryland. The people who taught the creative writing classes there were not people who would be known, but there was a fellow by the name of Herbert Schaumann who helped me a great, great deal. I dedicated my novel in part to him.

GRAHAM: Well, then he meant something to you. . . .

MEWSHAW: He meant a great deal to me. He was a translator of classical literature. He was, therefore, very good with the technical aspects of writing.

GRAHAM: This is very interesting. I'm intrigued by the whole idea of translation. I don't want to cheapen it and call it an exercise for a beginning writer, but it would seem to me it would teach you a respect for the difficulty of "the word."

MEWSHAW: Mr. Schaumann would agree with you very much. He is a very slow worker and the reason he is so slow is because he is attempting to approximate something of the cadence of the prosody of classical literature rather than to transliterate it into English. He wants to capture the verses and meter it was written in.

GRAHAM: He wants it all?

MEWSHAW: Right, and I think that he attempted to teach me something of a reverence for language, for meaning and for form as well.

GRAHAM: Excuse me, Mike, but did you start as a poet by any chance? So many novelists do a bit of poetry before they move into prose.

MEWSHAW: I didn't, and I really can't say why. I never attempted any poetry. I think it would be a very difficult form for me to attempt to express myself in, and again, I can't say why. I know that what you say is true. Many young people do start out that way.

GRAHAM: Well, that fearful compression that poetry demands frightens me. For that matter, so does the short story. I think if I were to write, I'd go directly to the novel, myself, through a kind of intimidation. You did an undergraduate course, then, in creative writing at Maryland.

MEWSHAW: Yes, and then I came to the University of Virginia, where I worked under George Garrett for a year. When George left to take over the writing program at Hollins, Peter Taylor arrived. It's an amusing thing. Peter Taylor, of course, is best known for his short stories, and he was interested in seeing short stories. I had written two novels, and he recommended that I write some short stories instead, so that it would make it easier for us to talk about my work. And I agreed with what you just said, that the compression demanded of a short-story writer made it difficult and also extremely demanding on a young writer who perhaps wasn't as sure of himself as he should have been. But Peter did insist that I write some short stories, and I think it was a great help to me—some of them have been accepted now, which was a surprise to me. But I think it was a better learning experience than anything else.

GRAHAM: Mike, am I correct in my memory that while you were turning out lots of pages of fiction, you were carrying a full load, were you not, as a graduate student in English? And you have your doctorate, don't you?

MEWSHAW: Yes, I do. I didn't take the creative writing program. I took the regular program in English literature.

GRAHAM: One thing that confuses me, and I know it's affected me—I'm not talented, I can't write—but let me ask this. Here you're spending "X" hours a day, doing your very best to turn out some fine prose yourself, and then "X" hours a day reading the masterpieces of English and American literature. Now, of course you learned from these, I'm sure, something about your own potential. But isn't that intimidating for the young writer? I mean, if you read Faulkner all afternoon, it must be a little hard for Mike Mewshaw to sit down and be free of Faulkner, or for that matter even to try to write prose?

MEWSHAW: I can understand how that could be a problem, but it didn't work that way with me. If anything, I think the grandeur of a man like Faulkner, or someone like Henry James, provided an inspiration to attempt, not to equal them, but to attempt to do anything. Where graduate work and study of literature might hurt is when you begin to emphasize various critical approaches to the literature, which then become so analytical and at times desiccated, dry, even sterile, that it'll hinder you in your own development as a writer, make you too analytical. It would change your approach from an organic one to one that emphasized symbolism or the other sort of graduate-school jargon.

GRAHAM: I've talked with many teachers of creative writing, and I realize that this is a personal position that every man would have to work out for himself, but some teachers clearly emphasize form, a high, high consciousness on the part of a writer, while others are inclined to a sort of schizoid position, and emphasize unconsciousness with a later return of consciousness in rewriting. Have you got any method, any feeling on this sort of thing? You will be teaching creative writing at the University of Massachusetts. How do you expect to deal with that?

MEWSHAW: If you are directing that question particularly at teaching young writers, I think I would emphasize first a conscious technique. I think too many young writers spend a great deal of their time trying to express some deep, dark, vague, amorphous reaction to their own experience of youth, and I personally think it would be more beneficial to focus on, perhaps a personal experience, but a smaller experience, one that they can come to grips with in a conscious fashion, and shape.

GRAHAM: Not "life," but a birthday party when you were twelve, that kind of thing?

MEWSHAW: I think that's a more logical approach. I know that in every creative writing class I ever took there was always a very talented, but perhaps undisciplined fellow, who was writing a book of a thousand pages, a book that was going to encompass all of human experience. And inevitably it broke down, and that writer despaired of accomplishing what he had set out to do. I don't think you can go from a senior in high school to James Joyce. I think that there are a lot of steps in between, that you have to climb those stairs.

GRAHAM: I should imagine "virtues" like patience, tenacity, and maybe just plain raw courage are tools needed, perhaps even before talent, in being a writer.

MEWSHAW: Well, I think so. You've named three qualities I think are inseparable from talent. It's assumed that anybody who wants to be a writer, or succeeds as a writer even to a limited extent, has a certain amount of talent. But if he doesn't have patience, which I think is perhaps the best quality a writer can have, I don't think he'll last. For one thing a great deal of patience is needed just in dealing with the brute facts of publishing, dealing with agents, that sort of thing. Also you have to sit and wait for the muse, for the word. You mentioned courage, too, and this is something that perhaps sounds fatuous for anyone to say after Hemingway said it so often and Mailer keeps repeating it; but I would emphasize not physical courage, but internal courage. A writer, as he proceeds with his career, kills himself at the same time. He kills his talent by letting go of it, he puts it on the page and then he can't do it again. It's like shedding a skin every time he writes a book. All of us have just so many skins though some of us are bigger than others. There's a kind of deeply poignant feeling about writing a book and letting it go, because that's part of you that's gone and it's not there to call on again.

GRAHAM: It would seem to me, involved with that, a great deal of what you must do constitutes a severe stretching of your memory as well as your imagination, so that you've got to go into everything that's happened to you, at least by indirection, do you not? And that's scary. Don't you have to understand more clearly, to be a writer, say, your relations with a girl in the second year of high school, or your father at a baseball game?

MEWSHAW: I would say so. I think that you have to be able to see your own experiences in a way that most people don't see their own experiences, and perhaps the greatest difficulty is then, once you've seen those experiences, to distill from them a fictional construct. You have to understand the meaning and be able to abstract if from the raw material of that experience. Memory helps, imagination helps, and then the blending of the two is what makes literature, I think.

GRAHAM: And that weird sense that you are implying of being strongly moved by the facts of your life, and yet needing to get some kind of distance through form to a fictional construct rather than just an outpouring.

MEWSHAW: I think it's an interesting thing, what you've probably observed, interviewing so many writers, knowing them, they're a strange alchemy of sentimentalists and hard-nosed people.

GRAHAM: Fine, that is what I see in them.

MEWSHAW: And they can see the facts. They're very incisive about the facts, but it also is commonly known that they're deeply affected by those facts. They can neither be too hard-nosed about the facts nor can they be too sentimental. If they want to be successful, there has to be a proper balance.

7. JAMES SEAY

Born 1939 in Panola County, Mississippi. Educated at the University of Mississippi and the University of Virginia. Has taught at Virginia Military Institute and the University of Alabama. Presently Associate Professor of English at Vanderbilt University.

Book: (poetry) *Let Not Your Hart* (1970).

JAMES SEAY

(Vanderbilt University)

I really hope that I don't quell any kind of talent, and I don't really think you can. I think that the person who is going to write is going to do that despite anything you can do for or against them.

GRAHAM: Jim, you are teaching poetry writing, you're not involved with the fiction end?

SEAY: Not here at Hollins. At Alabama I do teach some fiction writing, although my claim to expertise there is rather shaky.

GRAHAM: Even with that shaky base, do you see the real principles as essentially different? Are there higher principles that are going to function well for either?

SEAY: Well, there are some aspects that overlap. Sometimes, say, for instance, the matter of point of view will come up in a poem, and of course you know it's crucial in fiction; and it's not something you think a lot about in poetry. And often a student has an idea, a concept that involves a narrative, the narrative mode.

GRAHAM: In some of your own musing poems in your book, *Let Not Your Hart,* it seems to me I see novelistic techniques, at least in the sense

59

of point of view that you brought up, where different people are reminiscing about different things. It may be Jim Seay of 1945 who's doing the talking in a given poem, but you've got, as Jim Seay of 1970, you've got to adjust. With the poets, now, that you work with, you're in a very particular teaching position. It's different from my usual teaching position, in that the students that come to you must have—they're preselected, or self-selected—they must have an image of what they want to become. Do you do anything with young writers about that image?

SEAY: Not really. I think my experience—and it's not been a lengthy one—I've only been teaching four years now full-time—with the students I've come across, I've found that it's best to try to let the student find his own direction. About all that I can offer is some suggestion of shortcuts. Often this is a matter of techniques. I can tell him about the publishing scene, what he can expect in that. Often, you feel yourself wondering if maybe you shouldn't discourage a student; although colleagues of mine, of late, decided that anywhere we see a glimmer of promise, we're going to praise and praise, because sometimes a student may be a slow developer. At the end of four years something just breaks, and the language opens up. It's something, for me, intuitive, if I think someone has promise of writing good poetry or good fiction, it's something intuitive. It's both his approach to language and an approach to life.

GRAHAM: A poet first of all has to be a madman as far as language is concerned. Doesn't he just have to plain love language and the attempt, at least, to pat it into shape?

SEAY: Yes, and you sense this in these students, as I say, that have promise. I'm not making writing out totally as a gift, but there are those students and you sense in the way they approach language as a joy. They pick up word-plays, and they're more interested in etymologies and resonances of words, and all of that. It's that that I look for, and those are the ones that I'm most enthusiastic about. I really hope that I don't quell *any* kind of talent, and I don't really think you can. I think that the person who is going to write is going to do that despite anything you can do for or against them.

GRAHAM: You've got to be pretty hard-headed, don't you, to persist in writing? It's just too tough.

SEAY: It'd be interesting to know just how many writers have persevered just for spite.

GRAHAM: In justifying what you feel is an intuition on your part—as you described this sort of passion for manipulating words, interest in etymology and what-have-you—have you ever speculated (your firstborn is now in your household) have you ever speculated on the teaching of writing of poetry to the very young? You now get people when you could argue that they are what they are, at age of eighteen.

SEAY: Yes, and their sense of language is perhaps already formulated, set.

GRAHAM: Or unformulated. . . .

SEAY: Or lacking. Personally, I'm not, though there's been some interest in this lately, in New York, by a poet named Kenneth Koch. In fact, there's an anthology of poems just been published, all of them taking rise from this program in which perhaps pre-school children, at least children in the lower grades, were taken into this special class, and they were encouraged to write poetry. And some of their images and the things they came up with are just really a pleasure to read.

GRAHAM: I spun through, admittedly, I didn't go page by page, an anthology called *Miracles*.

SEAY: I don't know that.

GRAHAM: Well, I'm almost tempted to say to you, Jim, as a poet, you don't want to read that, because they're written by children. And some of them are so good they knock you down.

SEAY: It's an interesting thing: what does this experience do to the child's mind? Does it set it up for something, some potential for development? My own child, what if I began at a very early age for him, perhaps reading to him, and then, when he got a sense of language, encouraging him to deal with images or think about metaphors or figurative language, and just see what came to the mind? Would it be creating a situation there, a condition which could be developed?

GRAHAM: One thing I've discovered with my children is that I think it's natural in children to thrust toward metaphor because their vocabulary is limited. I can remember my daughter referring to the "bone" of a watermelon, meaning the rind. She did not know the word "rind," but she knew that this was the part that went away as the bone of a chicken.

SEAY: Kind of an inside-out bone.

GRAHAM: Have you discovered any correlation between music and poetry within your students' background or your own for that matter?

SEAY: In my own case, I'm not trained in music. I have utterly no knowledge of music theory. I play to an inner ear in my poetry. And it may be musical and it may be lyrical and it may not. I do think that there are some lyrical qualities in some of it. But one of my best students, for example, is trained in music, started at an early age at the piano and worked himself up and is in a rock band. Whether that carries over into his poetry, I cannot say. I've got other students from, say, rural backgrounds without any training in music who are equally good.

GRAHAM: What crossed my mind was the vast number of poets who are also amateur painters or, before writing, were painters; and the whole idea of the interrelation of the arts as part of the training for the poet is a tease at least.

SEAY: I've put a lot of time in galleries. And any time I go to a city, my first thought is to go to some art museum. You know, if I'm in New York I immediately think of the Museum of Modern Art or the Metropolitan. In Chicago, I'm especially fond of the Art Institute. They have a grand collection of the Impressionists.

GRAHAM: How, from your experience as teacher and within your experience as man, do you then urge your students—you mentioned art and life—do you urge your students to experience widely in the arts in order to be sharper observers of life? So many of your own poems, for instance, start with an eye observation. The data is there. Is this the sort of thing you try to urge your students toward?

SEAY: No, I would tell any of them, of course, to try and get some "couth," but I don't find myself urging any of them to try sketching or drawing, but we talk. Now, with this generation that you're teaching, you find yourself making analogies to the cinema. Also I try to make a point with reference to a painting, a piece of sculpture. I don't do this much with music because I just don't know it that well.

GRAHAM: Do you see special exercises as necessary and valuable, do you have them?

SEAY: Exercises, say, conventional poetic forms? I tried that earlier and the results were disastrous. I said, write a sonnet—any kind of sonnet, it can Petrarchan or Elizabethan, whatever you want to do, or you can try to violate any of these conventional sonnet forms. This was with beginning students, and I think maybe at times I've had them do these exercises, I've had maybe one or two sonnets out of fifty that are worth reading.

8. JAMES WHITEHEAD

Born 1936 in St. Louis, Missouri. Educated at Vanderbilt University. Has taught at the University of Iowa and Millsaps College. Currently Associate Professor of English and co-director of the Writing Program at the University of Arkansas.

Books: (poetry) *Domains* (1966); (novel) *Joiner* (1971).

JAMES WHITEHEAD

(University of Arkansas)

We've sort of lost the sense of music except in the hands of some of the really old practitioners and, very predictably, in the hands of a man like, say, Frost, who had a classical education.

GRAHAM: Now, essentially, Jim, you teach the writing of poetry, don't you? Or do you range into fiction?

WHITEHEAD: I happen to be teaching the writing of poetry right now at the University of Arkansas. My interest is about equally divided between poetry and fiction.

GRAHAM: Is there any basic difference in trying to teach young students—or for that matter to mature students—are there basic moves that you would make in teaching poetry that you would not make in teaching prose? I have difficulty seeing that there's any real difference.

WHITEHEAD: It seems to me there are a few differences. Let me give you a little background on the way we set it up, at least at Arkansas. The workshop, of course, is a pretty freewheeling situation, in which the fiction writers and poets have their manuscripts printed on mimeograph paper and stapled together, and then we distribute them three or four days before the weekly three-hour meeting. Then everyone has read it, in other words edited it, the manuscript. For that, in fact, is what it works off as, an editing session.

GRAHAM: Both students and staff are in this three-hour meeting?

WHITEHEAD: Right, once a week, and this works out pretty well. I discovered from being in workshops as a student—several places, most especially at the University of Iowa—that there was a little difficulty with a common ground for vocabulary, and in knowledge of certain traditions and modalities in both poetry and fiction. Now this is a little more acute in poetry, of course; for the terminology of poetry is a little more ancient and a little more complex, by way of being derivative from Latin and Greek sources. The terminology of metaphor and prosody is very ancient. Now I don't happen to believe that the words that have been passed down to us in those areas are sacrosanct in any way at all, but I feel like students should know them. And I was glad I went out and made myself learn them so I had a frame of reference to work around in.

GRAHAM: Well, I would argue, say, the first two months in a college physics course consists of learning some definitions. What is an ohm?

WHITEHEAD: Right. The first semester students come into our program they take—at the same time they're in the first semester of workshop—a course called "Form and Theory of Poetry" if they are in poetry workshop. They take "Form and Theory of Fiction" if they are in fiction workshop. I have taught, the last couple of years, "Form and Theory of Poetry." I'm going to teach "Form and Theory of Fiction" pretty soon. The idea there is to study the problems of point of view, genre, metaphor, and prosody. It's a very intensive course, and I'm sorry to say it's a rather academic course, the idea being, we're going to learn this, and then we can do anything we want to.

GRAHAM: You're not trying to lock them in on any kind of form or anything.

WHITEHEAD: Absolutely not, absolutely not. In fact, the truism is correct, which is that if a person knows the history of form, and understands the problems of particular genres, and understands the problems of metaphor, he has many more options than he would have otherwise.

GRAHAM: One of the things that it would seem to me that you've got to do, even with a young writer, or maybe essentially with a young writer, is to let him really understand he has options, that a given line, just because it's done this way, does not have to be done that way.

WHITEHEAD: It's really amazing how we find people who are genuinely talented in handling one dimension of poetry, say, a person who is writing a kind of Imagist poem, has a fairly comfortable sense of what a line is, intuitively breaks the line, puts together wonderfully fresh and sometimes bizarre images, and yet obviously has no sense of the possibility of using the phonic strata of a poem for support for images—just really never heard of it. Now, I happen to think that this is partially a result of the very intensive work done by the New Critics in the semantics of literature for about the last thirty years. And I think they overcompensated in that direction because they were afraid of linguistic philosophers or something like that, in the twenties and thirties. But we've sort of lost the sense of music except in the hands of some of the really old practioners and, very predictably, in the hands of a man like, say, Frost, who had a classical education. Now, if I find a first-rate surrealist poet, who handles a sort of flat line very comfortably, I would never say to him, necessarily, write a villanelle or a sestina, or try to write in blank verse using the traditional devices. I would never tell a person who handles a kind of traditional, metaphysical conceit to stop doing that and write monologues. But if he shows me a poem in the workshop, and this poem is really bending itself in the direction of a mode that this person is not particularly gifted in, then he might have the option, having had it introduced to him. And we sort of say, "Well, why don't you try it this way?"

GRAHAM: Certainly, in reading, over the past few weeks, a great deal of work by younger poets, I suddenly realized that there's an essential difference between a poem that is written, in effect, out of memory as the poet looks back at something, puts it in front of you—*but in memory*—through his images, and the poet who is using the point of view of "it is happening now and is before me."

WHITEHEAD: Right, one of the least understood things about poetry is the matter of point of view. You asked me earlier if there were any carry-overs between fiction and poetry. Of course, there are. The only real difference is that the vocabulary and terminology of fiction is much more recent, historically, than it is in poetry. But one of the things in poetry that we fail to understand many times is that the verb tense has a radical effect on the perception of the reader, in the way it comes into his consciousness. We are beginning to understand that there is something almost philosophically different between the recollection and the *monologue,* which achieves a kind of immediacy, which isn't necessarily better than recollection, but certainly very different. And for the purposes of a poet it requires a different kind of execution. A writer is a performer. He is performing in the language and he is trying to predict his effects, to a great extent, on his audience. I don't mean he calculates this during a first draft, or necessarily becomes highly conscious of this in a second draft. But at some point or another he becomes aware of his audience, and begins to calculate effects to one extent or another.

GRAHAM: Well, back to something you brought up right at the start. He's got to figure, just as you with your students have to figure, what is the common ground. He's got to find some common counters or he's not going to be able to get at us at all.

WHITEHEAD: And if we just understand these, if we do see writing as a performance and the writer as one who is trying to communicate, and he's got certain techniques by which he can do it, then he'll begin to write pretty well, probably. One other problem, I'd like to say that in the process of teaching, of teaching writing, I don't think you can teach writing—that is a truism. I teach reading, and I teach reading the way writers read. In other words you can't inspire, you can't make a person disgorge brilliant images, you can't make a person suddenly have a great sense of natural rhythm, you can't do any of those things. All you can do is edit. All you can do is proliferate the possibilities for this talent, and this is done by thorough reading. Most people cannot read worth a damn.

GRAHAM: I argue this with my graduate students in straight academic courses.

WHITEHEAD: See, I don't think, again, I don't think there are "straight academic" courses. And that is a term that I really don't like. There are scholars who do research, and there are techniques for research, and this is a great thing. However, most of our research should be intended to create graceful readers, readers who can comprehend and enjoy at all levels of the consciousness, with the ability to receive the emotional dimension of a piece of literature, but also to enjoy the composition and structure of it simultaneously.

GRAHAM: I can delight in that definition, since no matter what I teach, I'm teaching reading. One thing that now teases me. With the reading that you have your students doing, there's always the danger that the young person may wind up falling in love with a writer and, either consciously or unconsciously becoming imitative. But the thing that I'm teased by is the problem of the young writer fighting with and for his craft, becoming intimidated by the—well, by the *success*, if you will, of great writing. Do you find that as a sort of psychological problem?

WHITEHEAD: Well, what do you mean by success of great writing? Do you mean he has a professor who says that William Butler Yeats is a god? Something like that?

GRAHAM: Or the student *sees* him as a god and blocks him, Yeats blocking the student, because the student realizes, "Well, I can't do that."

WHITEHEAD: Okay, right, I think I know what you were getting into there. It's something like this: there are a few writers that almost inevitably overwhelm you. However, one of the things you begin to teach a person—or rather you begin to release in him, allow him to understand—is that there is a great deal of pleasure in reading good writers, not just reading the great writers.

9. SYLVIA WILKINSON

Born 1940 in Durham, North Carolina. Educated at the University of North Carolina at Greensboro, Hollins College, and Stanford University. Has taught at Asheville-Biltmore College and William and Mary. Presently on writing staff of the University of North Carolina at Chapel Hill.

Books: (novels) *Moss on the North Side* (1966), *A Killing Frost* (1967), *Cale* (1970).

SYLVIA WILKINSON

(University of North Carolina
at Chapel Hill)

I went through a long period of writing
things about watching people from
the waist down, and I actually had this
vision of this. I do this with my students
artificially. I make them imagine the world
from the point of view of a cockroach
about to be stepped on. . . .

GRAHAM: Sylvia, about this whole business of teaching writing, I know that you did work as a student in creative writing at Hollins and then at Stanford and also Greensboro. What does all this add up to? I'm not going to get caught simplistically in the trap of, "You can't teach or learn creative writing." And yet—let's try this. What did your training mean to you as novelist? What did it "do for you"? Or, "what did they do to you"?

WILKINSON: When I first started writing, I was only twelve years old, and I tried to get some kind of response in the public school system. And I found out very early that this was a sort of hopeless thing. You do as you're told in the public school system, and I was twenty-one years old and a good long ways into a novel before I really reached a creative writing class with

71

Randall Jarrell. At this time I received from the creative writing class and the creative writing teacher what I needed, and that was simply reinforcement, exposure, criticism, because I was in a stage of almost complete isolation.

GRAHAM: You needed a working world to live in, really.

WILKINSON: Exactly. I had no one to bounce my work off of but my friends, my family, and people who had no reason to be terribly critical of my work.

GRAHAM: Or to be able to suggest what some possible options for change might be.

WILKINSON: And I think most people, when they don't have the benefit of a creative writing class, tend to write very conventional sort of stuff. They think everything has to be in a third-person narrative voice.

GRAHAM: And that's interesting, because one of the tempting things about the novel of yours I've just finished reading, *A Killing Frost*—right there, it's first person, but not just first person remembering, but first person seeing. It's that present tense that I think gets some of your effects. And I guess if a young writer doesn't realize that he can either see or remember, for instance . . .

WILKINSON: Yeah, well . . . The interesting thing about that is that I looked back at a rough draft the other day—giving it to a student who's doing a master's thesis—and I realized that I wrote that first chapter five times and four of those times were in third person before I realized what I really wanted was to be able to just talk in my own voice and to watch things unfold in front of me, rather than just unfold in the past. The present tense—I didn't realize I was using it until I got about halfway through the book. It's probably a good thing. It's a very difficult tense when you become conscious of it.

GRAHAM: With five rewritings of the first chapter of *A Killing Frost*, and four of them in the third person, are you suggesting that maybe—a simple hypothesis—but maybe, if you had been working at that time with a creative writing person, they might have suggested, "Sylvia"—after the second rewriting, "try this"?

WILKINSON: Well, it's a funny thing how that happened. I was at Stanford University at that time, and I had been having a certain problem with my writing teacher out there, Wallace Stegner. He was somewhat bothered by my destruction of the English language, and the fact that I rarely write a subordinate sentence. Everything's like a telephone conversation, connected by and's, then's, and but's, you know. So he kept bugging me about this and I was getting so self-conscious I couldn't write. I was reaching the point where I was just going to write and tell him this is the way an illiterate Southern girl talks. And the only way to get away with that was first person. So, in a way, my negative response to the teacher was what I needed rather than a positive response.

GRAHAM: But, as you said, you've got to have somebody to bounce it off of.

WILKINSON: Bounce it off of. Because most of us have an idea of our story, we have an idea of our character, but what really makes for good writing is figuring out *how* to tell that story. Most of the students I've worked with, and most of the students I've seen in classes are struggling for the "how." It's not a new story; it's just "how" they tell it.

GRAHAM: Back to *A Killing Frost* and this idea of "how." I've read, maybe ten volumes of poems by young poets in the past ten days. And it does seem to me you younger writers are becoming more and more conscious of this idea of voice. I don't quite mean point of view, that's too handy; because point of view is perhaps an intellectual judgment, but voice is either a psychological or an aesthetic one. I guess I could go through those volumes and find that almost every poet, every one of the poets has written a poem about voice, or the still voice, or two voices—this kind of thing, with this "how" that you're talking about.

WILKINSON: And I, following along that same line, think writing, when you're a young writer, you know, is so much experimentation. You're looking for your own way of doing things. You don't really know it yet. And in my new novel I use, I think, eight different voices, eight different people, and I work within their heads, frequently viewing the same event from different people.

GRAHAM: I've just finished reading Shelby Foote's *Follow Me Down*, and he does this with enormous success. And then that triggered me to recalling Joyce Cary and the wonderful trilogy of *Herself Surprised, To Be a Pilgrim* and *The Horse's Mouth*. Now, let me corner you on this. Do you lose your nerve—I guess you must often lose your nerve when you're writing—but what happens to you when you know you need a certain character and yet you have that sticky sense that you can't get inside his or her mind? Are you just going to have to opt out? Is that a dead-end question?

WILKINSON: Well, yes and no. I reached that sticky situation in this new novel, and I found myself—it's really a tremendous exercise of the creative imagination. For instance, never having had a child, I had to work through the mind of a woman who was having a baby at this time. You piece together all your information and you filter it out through your imagination. Now I would not be afraid to attempt to imagine what it would be like to have a child. I have a boy in this new novel, and I wanted to have him go to a burlesque show; so I went to a burlesque show and took notes. This is my fictional research. Then I took all the information and filtered it through this boy's mind, but I will be the first to admit that the Negro boy in this book is one that I won't do that to, because I'm just not ready. I just don't know enough, and I don't have that kind of guts. I don't have that kind of information. But I think I can give him a fair shake in the book by simply watching his responses and watching how other people respond to him.

GRAHAM: Well, let me ask you this, in terms of research and experience, really—memory—I think it was R. V. Cassill of Brown University who said that in the act of examining your memory, there are so many discoveries that you make that memory somehow changes into imagination, almost—is this your experience?

WILKINSON: This has always been something that's fascinated me. I work so much with memory. I like a period of ten years between my characters, like the boy I'm writing about now—he's ten years younger than myself. Memory—once something becomes memory then it can become part of your imagination. Your imagination can act upon it in just a tremendously different way. And another thing here, memory becomes better. It's almost like physical exercise; you learn to jump better if you jump more every day. And I first started out only being able to remember how I felt as a child of seven, but now I actually recall just with really very accurate detail walking in the woods with my grandfather when I was four, a sickness I had when I was four and a half, this kind of thing. It increases, it's almost like self-hypnosis, I guess. You just get better and better at it.

GRAHAM: In line with memory, then, you're saying then that writing is a very intricate form of self-discovery, of trying to pull together things. Not unlike, I guess, psychoanalysis, as you're going back trying to find the things that happened to you that are still in your memory and in some kind of a new context really, *because* you remember them.

WILKINSON: Because it's retrospect. You know that if they're there, then something planted them there, something, you know. For instance, a child walking with a grandfather at four: I suddenly see this new perspective, I see his knees. I went through a long period of writing things about watching people from the waist down, and I actually had this vision of this. I do this with my students artificially. I make them imagine the world from the point of view of a cockroach about to be stepped on, and how does he dodge the feet. But if you really work at it you can do it in your own life and get this perspective, because . . . I guess that's where imagination and memory do merge, the two things come together.

GRAHAM: Because then you can take, in a sense, anything. The imagination, if it takes a chunk of memory and puts it in another context, then that is the enormous act or part of the enormous act of imagination.

WILKINSON: If you write, like you say, from this self-discovery thing—I write almost totally without a plan. I make my plan as I go along. I'm like the student who makes the outline after he finishes the paper, because the teacher says, write an outline. I think that's the most valid way to write. These students say, "Ah, I wrote the outline after I finished the paper, Miss Wilkinson," and I say, "That's very good, that's the best way to organize what you've said, and also the outline doesn't get in your way when you're trying to write."

GRAHAM: You mean if a character starts to really open up on you . . .?

WILKINSON: Right.

GRAHAM: Do you start a novel—have you ever started a novel about one person and suddenly realized that it was really about someone else?

WILKINSON: About someone else? In *A Killing Frost*, in many ways, I was writing about my grandmother, but it ended up being as much about Ramie.

GRAHAM: Oh, indeed, indeed. That tension is evident in the book, and I was afraid for a good while that it might be a novel in praise of the grandmother totally. And I was delighted as the novel progressed to see you followed the other characters down.

WILKINSON: And I didn't really know, when I started that book, I would have been completely at a loss to explain the conflict between the child and the grandmother. But when I let it unfold, when I let it just happen, then I was able not to let an outline get in my way, and was able to make some tremendous discoveries. Also, if I knew where a book was going, I'd be really bored.

2. Frequently you uncover some things that you almost wish you hadn't. Sometimes some things frighten you very much.

GRAHAM: Sylvia, what have you got to say to me in terms of reading? Who are you reading that I might read? Do you do a lot of reading? Is this part of your world as writer?

WILKINSON: It's a funny thing. I feel like I read constantly, and yet, I'm never really able to keep up with what is going on today. I go through periods where I really make an effort to read certainly all the books written by friends of mine. Then I go back to reading old things . . . reading Dostoevsky and rereading Dostoevsky, reading Eudora Welty and rereading her.

GRAHAM: I think rereading is one of the great pleasures. That's the pleasure of the connoisseur. Any man can enjoy a book once. It's when you do that second reading that the reading begins.

WILKINSON: I get bogged down in books. I find myself reading a paragraph over and over and saying, "Oh, what a splendid paragraph! Isn't it beautiful? I wish I could do that." And it just takes me forever to get through a book.

GRAHAM: What you're describing right there is perhaps a necessary hazard of your profession as writer. When you find something good, there must be some question of "how did he pull that off?"

WILKINSON: It works that way with something bad, too. Because I'm a creative writing teacher I read a paragraph, and I say, "There's something wrong, what did he do wrong?" So you spend so much of your time almost exhausting your creative imagination on someone else's writings.

GRAHAM: This is a whole new world for me, really, because I've often wondered how a writer reads and you may have explained it. When you're reading, does it throw you off? Do you see things? Does it depress you, can't you see things there that you suspect strongly that Sylvia Wilkinson can't do and will never be able to do?

WILKINSON: Oh, no, no . . . I love to sit at the feet of a master. When I read Eudora Welty, I just sigh. I need heroes. I think everybody needs heroes. This is one thing that is very sad about my students. I always give them a little test at the first of the year and I say, "Who are your heroes?" Or "Who were your heroes five years ago?" And so frequently, they don't have any. They did have them, they used to have them.

GRAHAM: This opens what is a fascinating thing to me. It seems that a lot of people—I can't help but suspect that some of them are your students, I know that I'm one of those people—I think that they would like to *be* writers, but are not prepared to become writers. Do you have problems in your teaching of creative writing, not so much the "how," the "craft" of writing, but in clarifying for students what it means to *be* a writer? You lead a different life.

WILKINSON: I went into teaching probably more bright-eyed than I should have. Such a small, tiny percentage of your students even put the amount of effort on a manuscript that you do. It's so depressing, spending hours and hours in your office working over a manuscript with a student. And then you suddenly realize, he had the ability, but he didn't have the energy. He didn't have the stamina, he just didn't have that "stick-with-it-ism."

GRAHAM: You're suggesting, are you not, not only psychological energy and stamina, but physical energy and stamina? The ability to hang in, sitting on the first four inches of your chair?

WILKINSON: And to make yourself work when you really don't feel like it and all these things. Just the business of discipline. And lots of teachers, Randall Jarrell was one of them . . . he was a magnificent teacher. He was my teacher. He used to identify so totally.

GRAHAM: He was so warm. I met him on one very memorable occasion and I was, within thirty seconds, talking with a friend.

WILKINSON: Oh yes. When you told him about a particular struggle you had, not only with your book, but with your school work and with your home life and all this, he would identify so totally with your struggle that you were almost sorry that you mentioned it because you hurt him. He hurt for you. A really good writing teacher is able to identify with a student's struggle. And a really good editor does this. And I hope that my students will become good editors.

GRAHAM: This is interesting because, in my observation, I think that Peter Taylor is much as you describe. He gives of himself so much.

WILKINSON: One of my heroes!

GRAHAM: Splendid, you're picking the right people. In working with young writers, would you consciously have them read biographies of writers, just to see that Trollope got up and wrote, Lamb wasn't very well, and had his mad sister and so forth?

WILKINSON: Another way of doing this is to show them manuscripts. There are books that come out now that, for instance, show the early drafts of famous writers' work, like William Styron's first draft of something. And Kay Boyle is a wonderful example. She'll write the same paragraph eight times. And I show these to my students, just to show them the evolution.

GRAHAM: This stuff doesn't pop full-born from their brows.

WILKINSON: And everybody's different. Eudora Welty in her manuscripts will maybe only change one or two words, whereas Kay Boyle would rewrite, rewrite, and rewrite. And I hope this communicates to them this self-knowledge. You find out your own creative process.

GRAHAM: And you must become rather a different person, not only in terms of the creative process of the craft of writing. At the end of the novel, you must be a different person than you were at the beginning.

WILKINSON: You scare yourself sometimes, too. Frequently you uncover some things that you almost wish you hadn't. Sometimes some things frighten you very much. For instance, you write a novel and you see a recurring preoccupation with death as I saw in *A Killing Frost*, and I didn't see this until I wrote it down on paper. So, it's a self-discovery that, like lots of self-discoveries, is not without its fear.

GRAHAM: The pain of self knowledge. . . . With students, how long is it profitable, almost, for them to be in a writing program? I'm sure it must be healthy to be around others who are struggling to find the same things that you are struggling to find, but are they apt to talk each other out, or are they apt to end up seeing you as not only, to go to your term, as ''hero,'' but as mother, daddy, crutch?

WILKINSON: Ultimately, they may depend on you too much. This is, I think, a very interesting question. I am a product of creative writing programs. One day, I suddenly felt my wings, and I took off. But, I still keep a close contact with some of my very beloved teachers like Louis Rubin, and I have five or six people that I still show my work to. But I no longer need this class, this massive group. But with students? Yes, I think you're right. So many of them become dependent on you. They become dependent on this class. This is a touchy subject. I'm not too sure we've solved it yet. But, I tell them over and over again that the most hurting thing is that when you suddenly expose a book to the world, you no longer have sympathetic criticism. People in a writing class are thinking in terms of "how can I make this better?" You lose that. It's gone. It's a very sad day.

GRAHAM: I guess that it's a necessary nest, then, while you are experimenting, being foolish, or clumsy at best. I take it from what you are saying is that in a workshop students are generous with each other or kind or tactful or both?

WILKINSON: People who sit in on classes are constantly amazed at how sensitive and how very hard these kids are trying and because they know that, someday, they're going to be sitting there reading their story, the criticism is rarely destructive.

GRAHAM: If only through self-protection.

WILKINSON: As soon as you get one kid in the class who starts being very mean and very destructive, the day he reads you see him with his knees knocking against each other.

GRAHAM: What kind of other reading do you do?

WILKINSON: Well, right at the moment I'm fascinated with race drivers and with their motivation to race. I do a lot of talking, which is easier than reading. I read, of course, all the journals, and try to get my hands on the personal notes that they've written.

GRAHAM: You mean that you're the girl that stands in the drugstore reaching the high racks in the back for *Car and Driver*?

WILKINSON: *Hot Rod*! Well, actually, I have subscriptions to them all.

GRAHAM: Are you competent in technical matters? Do you know all about cams?

WILKINSON: Let's say I'm to the doctor what a nurse is. I'm a competent helper. My fascination with automobiles is like my fascination with the minute detail, the importance of not leaving a screw loose.

GRAHAM: Is this reading of these various automobile magazines, racing magazines, being funneled into your present work? Are you writing on it yet?

WILKINSON: No, not yet. I'm doing some articles. I have done one for *Sports Illustrated,* and I'm doing newspaper articles because I feel the necessity in sports. The public wants to know what this guy does in the pits, what he tells his pit crew. Does he get mad? Is he temperamental? I've got my hand on some of this information and I'm looking for the way to filter it out.

GRAHAM: The information will percolate and percolate, and one of these days there will be a Sylvia Wilkinson novel with grease on the face.

WILKINSON: Right. But, at the moment, it will take more nerve than I have. The race driver is an extremely complicated person, and the closer I get to all of this the more I realize how complicated he is.

10. JAMES DICKEY

Born 1923 in Atlanta, Georgia. Educated at Clemson and Vanderbilt University. Has taught at Rice University, University of Florida, Reed College, San Fernando Valley State, University of Wisconsin. Presently Professor of English at the University of South Carolina.

Books: (poetry) *Into the Stone* (1960), *Drowning with Others* (1962), *Helmets* (1964), *Two Poems of the Air* (1964), *Buckdancer's Choice* (1965), *Poems 1957–1967 (1967)*, *Eye-Beaters, Blood, Victory, Madness, Buckhead, and Mercy* (1970); (novel) *Deliverance* (1970); (nonfiction) *Babel to Byzantium* (1968), *Self-Interviews* (1970), *Sorties* (1971).

JAMES DICKEY

(University of South Carolina)

I try to throw as wide a net as I can, and the intention being to open up as many potentialities to them as I can do in the given time limit.

GRAHAM: Jim, I remain fascinated with this whole problem of what you're doing here at the Hollins Conference. How do you go at these very much self-selected students in terms of teaching writing, whether it be poetry or prose? And you've done both.

DICKEY: Well, I look on it as kind of a fearful responsibility because if you teach a course in poetry, you're really not doing only that. Because poetry is not abstracted from life, from existence and from experience; so really, if you're attempting to teach a course on the writing of poetry, you're really teaching a course in living in the world and in attempting to say something about it.

GRAHAM: Certainly your own poems are long, they are intricate, they are demanding on yourself. I mean, this is nakedly evident in your poetry, and I know you can't possibly be a father confessor totally or a guide to a lifestyle. I'm curious about the young person who perhaps may want more to *be* a writer than become one, you know.

DICKEY: There are really two kinds of people who think, say, in the early stages of their life that they want to write poetry. One kind wants more than to write, wants to be a writer. He thinks he likes or thinks he would like the distinction of being a writer. He likes the company of writers, he likes the whole ambience of writerdom.

GRAHAM: Certainly, from a distance, it looks like there's more fun than anything.

DICKEY: Yes, that's right, a community of free spirits, sensitive folks, and sort of an in-group. But those are inevitably the ones that are not going to be poets.

GRAHAM: They simply don't have the tenacity.

DICKEY: They don't like the thing for itself. The other category of writers, they like it. They like to write. I remember Mr. Auden once saying that he chose people for a creative writing class simply by asking them one question, "Why do you want to write poetry?" There are really only two categories of answers. One category is comprised of the people who say, "Look, I want to write poetry because I have important things to say." Those are the non-poets.

GRAHAM: Go ahead. That sounds like a reasonable reason.

DICKEY: The correct answer, according to Mr. Auden, is that when he asked the question, Why do you want to write poetry, the correct answer would be, "Well, I just like words. I like hanging around words, listening to words, and what they have to say. And trying to see what I can make them say."

GRAHAM: If you don't like one vowel sort of echoing another, and the consonants bumping, then you're in trouble.

DICKEY: If you don't like the thing itself, the actual doing of the thing and the making of the poem, regardless of whatever reputation it may bring you or whatever company it might put you in, desirable or undesirable, regardless of all those extraneous things. What the real poet concentrates on and loves is the doing of the thing itself, the making of the poem, his poem, his way.

GRAHAM: Now this brings me to something that it seems to me I've observed with poets in terms of looking at their own work. Your *Poems 1957–1967* is out. Can you let your poems alone in terms of this passion for manipulating language, for making, creating a world? Can you let your poems alone ten years after the fact or do you touch at them?

DICKEY: No, I don't. I make it a rule not to do that. I work on them so intensively for the time I do work on them, and when I turn loose of them I'm so sick of them, I never want to look at them again or deal with those specific problems that that poem raises ever again. I see one, say in an anthology, and I sort of, from a very great distance, judge it more or less objectively. I say, "Well, this was a pretty good idea that I botched." But I don't have any desire to go back and make a success of it. That's just something that I'd have chalk up as something I haven't been able to solve. On the other hand, sometimes I say, "Goodness, isn't that good? I wish I could write something that good now."

GRAHAM: With your students, what is your approach? Is it the carrot before the nose or the two-by-four with the nail, or do they have to do it themselves?

DICKEY: My approach is to attempt, with any given class, or with any given member of any given class, to try and isolate where his strength lies, and to bring that forth. And, to try to do something about his weaknesses. Any human writer has a certain number of things he can do well, more or less easily or instinctively, and a certain number of things that are difficult for him to do. We just try to bring out the things that he can do best and realize them to their fullest potential and try to minimize, or, if possible, with luck, eliminate the weaknesses.

GRAHAM: With your own poetry, I see it as dominated by an enormously strong sense of rhythm, *after* the observation—a very keen eye and ear for life, but then, I get this long thrust to your poems. You like a lot of room to operate in. Do you have your students exercise themselves in the various solutions to problems?

DICKEY: Yes, I do. I try to throw as wide a net as I can, and the intention being to open up as many potentialities to them as I can do in the given time limit.

GRAHAM: Will you give them—I want to use the word "force"—exercise? Would you have them, for instance, write a sonnet, or twenty lines of heroic couplets to test themselves?

DICKEY: Yes, sure. The way my classes are generally set up, I won't take on a student for less than a year, so the artificial boundaries of the semesters have to be utilized in some way. So what I do is to have the first semester in which I have them use all the received forms—the sonnet, the epigrammatic couplet, the heroic couplet, blank verse, some of the French forms like the sestina, and so on, to give them some kind of relatively thorough grounding in what has been done and how our forms have been used by other people. I have them attempt to adapt these to their own uses and their own subject matter. That's the first half of the year. We do nothing else but formal poems.

GRAHAM: Do they resist that exercise work?

DICKEY: Some of them do, but the good ones don't. They regard it as a challenge.

GRAHAM: Again, putting the words together to make a poem?

DICKEY: Yes.

GRAHAM: It's like playing football. You can't go outside the lines.

DICKEY: Or tennis.

GRAHAM: All right.

DICKEY: You can hit the greatest drive in the world, you know, but if it's out, it's out.

GRAHAM: And the referee is going to tell you about it.

DICKEY: You know it anyway, if you're a good player. But the second half of it is not that way at all. I just assume that there's a residue of information and technique carrying over from the first semester into the second semester. The whole second semester is taken up with each student writing one poem.

GRAHAM: Just one?

DICKEY: Just one, trying it lots of different ways.

GRAHAM: That's fascinating.

DICKEY: It is, it is. It turns out to be fascinating.

GRAHAM: The real depth plunge on this whole business of options.

DICKEY: Yes, options, attempting different things. Failing here, getting an inkling there, pursuing this, abandoning that.

GRAHAM: Is this poem a dramatic monologue or an epigram and you don't know yet, really?

DICKEY: It can be anything that they want. You don't know what it's going to be.

GRAHAM: Not to turn the cat o'nine tails on the master at this point, but do you ever exercise yourself formally that way, fighting for form?

DICKEY: Sure, sure. I have lots of sonnet sequences and things that I write. I'm not really very good as a formal poet, but I write them as a necessity of the discipline.

GRAHAM: In your own poetry, I keep seeing that you need room.

DICKEY: That seems to be so.

GRAHAM: You need to spread. Is this part of your thrust towards a long, musing poem that will have a key action in it?

DICKEY: I think so. I'm really not sure myself whether it's any kind of advantage to me to be overly reasonable or rational about my own motivations. So much of it is a matter of feeling with me, and what feels right rather than what I can justify intellectually.

GRAHAM: At times in your particular control—I think, almost over space—you wind up controlling a rhythm and that voice wants to go on talking, perhaps in reminiscence, perhaps in self-challenge. You seem to want to go over the banks.

DICKEY: I have a tendency to write longer than need be. This has been said by some of my critics. But the particular effects that I want to get cannot be achieved any other way.

GRAHAM: From time to time, do you run into students who feel they are already poets in the sense that they have already found their voice? Candidly, I'm wondering about the poets since Ginsberg's *Howl*.

DICKEY: Well, Ginsberg and those people . . . that's a chapter in the history of American sociology. It has nothing to do with poetry. The appeal of someone like Ginsberg or, on another level, Rod McKuen, is that they write the kind of poetry that their audience is capable of writing. In other words, it would be equally true to say not that all the little Ginsbergs write like Ginsberg, but that he writes like they do.

GRAHAM: In line with this, given the present situation with college students, are you getting a lot of protest poems? What I'm interested in, really, is the person who almost wants to use a poetic form for a manifesto. Are they shouting at you?

DICKEY: Oh, yes, there's an awful strong tendency to do that now, to use poetry as polemic or as propaganda of some sort for some cause. But the stuff is dead before it hits the paper. It's already dead.

GRAHAM: One of the great things, it seems to me, that you have to do is exercise tact with this sort of thing, to explain that the idea may be "relevant," but the poem doesn't exist.

DICKEY: You have to make it very plain to them that there is a very great difference between attempting to write an interesting phrase and saving the world.

11. WILLIAM HARRISON

Born 1933 in Dallas, Texas. Educated at Texas Christian University, Vanderbilt University, and the University of Iowa. Has taught at Atlantic Christian University and Iowa. Since 1964 has been Director of the Graduate Writing Program at the University of Arkansas.

Books: (novels) *The Theologian* (1965), *In a Wild Sanctuary* (1969), *Lessons in Paradise* (1971).

WILLIAM HARRISON

(University of Arkansas)

*We're very flexible. We don't want to get
people to write in any certain way. But
there are principles of good writing.*

GRAHAM: With this whole business of creative writing, I think one of
the really interesting things that is different from straight teaching is that
the students are self-selected, in a very particular way. They've already
tried, at least, to experience pretty fully. What do they expect to learn from
you? What are their expectations when they come in?

HARRISON: We have a lot of graduate students, and already they've
begun to write. And more frequently our writers in the graduate programs
and in creative writing programs around the country are twenty-seven or
twenty-eight years old.

GRAHAM: Oh, they're that old? Then, they've been around a little bit.

HARRISON: They've already got some experience behind them. And
their talent, of course, at times infects the undergraduate program at the
school. You also have a lot of precocious younger writers coming up on
campus.

GRAHAM: It's kind of nervy, is it not, for a person at twenty-seven or twenty-eight. I mean, I was committed to being a poet when I was twenty, but that's easy.

HARRISON: I think we have a cultural change, where everyone knows that he's not going to find his groove in life when he's twenty-one years old. I myself kicked around—I was in theological school when I was twenty-one, a far cry from what I'm doing now. And in between did several other kinds of things. I think we have a kind of new culture, where the young man, or the young woman, can drop out and find himself. This, of course, has been a very painful social experience through the years, for artists, but we have an affluent society in which this is more or less possible now.

GRAHAM: I know very often at the University of Virginia, one of my strongest temptations is to recommend that a young man simply drop out, no big deal, but go and pick peaches or what have you. Get some of this experience, maybe find himself.

HARRISON: The exciting thing, John, is that they do learn a lot about writing. I think one of the interesting things about the Hollins Conference is that so many people who are already talented go on to some greater concepts in writing—in fiction for example, the idea of the scene, the idea of the greater structure of stories and novels. Four of my students at the University of Arkansas in the last year and a half have published novels, each with a different publishing house. We've had an extraordinary scene at Arkansas for six years now. We're like Iowa—that was our predecessor—or Stanford. We find lots of young people out there who are ready to get in. The curriculum just proves that they're learning something, or doing something for themselves.

GRAHAM: The major test of a writing program, I would think—it would be so hard to measure—would be production. I'm fascinated with this age thing, because you are obviously dealing with people who have poked around enough. I would think they have a very strong, even fierce, commitment to learning everything they can out of writing. What do you do, however, with the people who have written a lot, and who may even be "fixed"? Can they profit, or are they stifled by their own egos?

HARRISON: What do you mean, "fixed"?

GRAHAM: Fixed in attitudes toward fiction, attitudes toward poetry. Are they willing to experiment with the instructor?

HARRISON: We're very flexible. We don't want to get people to write in any certain way. But there are principles of good writing. It begins with writing your grade school grammar text. You have to learn to write sentences, and then you go on and become a fiction writer as you begin to get a sense of the scene, the larger structures, and how to construct. We have a saying in creative writing—"You have to have a runner to teach you how to run." And indeed you do. And we have another saying, "Writing can't be taught, but it must be learned." So we have a lot of young people who are passionate to learn, are committed to learning and do learn. That's been proven. I think American literary education is beginning to change, John, under the impact of the influx of creative writing. For example, in art departments, in a usual-size university, you have eighteen or twenty practicing artists and a couple of art historians, whereas in English departments, traditionally, we have eighteen or twenty literary historians, and if lucky, one or two practicing writers. I think the balance has got to shift, and it will. Young people just aren't interested in going only into the pedagogical or teaching end of the English language. There's lots of communications, lots of industries devoted to communications, that need the young writer now. And creative writing is still a very open, and, at times, very profitable field.

GRAHAM: One man has argued that one of the real values of a creative writing course is that it makes a man a better reader.

HARRISON: That's true. We think, also, we turn out good teachers; because if you study the techniques and the form and organic nature of literature, of course, you simply become a better teacher. And the formalist approach to literary education is the one that our students are strong in.

GRAHAM: With these students, whether they are young or old, do you make them read much? Is this intrinsic in your writing course?

HARRISON: Oh, yes, and some of them resist it. You know, you get a lot of young writers who are sort of "To Hell with Grammar" writers, and you have a lot of young writers who resist reading. I had one student who quit the University of Arkansas because I wanted him to read *Anna Karenina* and the Russian names seemed to be long and difficult to pronounce. He may finally wind his way back into a writing career somewhere along the line, but he must embrace the Russians and what they did. Most of them go along with this reading program. I think we do make better readers, as well as some writers.

GRAHAM: One reason for my concern with this is that I know that I'm apt to think too highly of the great works. And I would hazard that, at least for some people, reading the masterworks of English or world literature would at least inhibit their own writing. Or is there enough ego to carry them through? Are they strongly enough convinced that they can learn?

HARRISON: We find that young writers are . . . (laughs) They have sufficient ego. But Joyce is not only a humbling experience, frequently a humiliating experience, but I think it helps them to come to terms with themselves.

GRAHAM: Do you have them imitate by any chance? It's a very old rhetorical technique.

HARRISON: I think good pedestrian writing is difficult, and really what you do with young people is get them up to a solid pedestrian state. Beyond that they're on their own. Whether they're going to become good stylists or master writers themselves is out of my hands. We, in a sense, bring them up to their first good recital; and the curious thing is that the publishing houses buy them at that level. And then the rest of their career is up to them. I'd hate to think that I didn't advance beyond my own first stories, first novel, and so it is with these students. They have to keep learning.

GRAHAM: The only way they can really learn is to write a great deal, is it not? I should think—back to the ego business—that one of your major problems is one of tact.

HARRISON: It's one of caring for the whole person in these programs. Frequently these older students that I was talking about come back to school, and in spirit they're young men. They're no longer as flexible as they once were. They don't want to be in the cramped academic environment, and you tell them, if you can be honest with them, at the first, that you know it's going to be difficult for them. And you paint as honest a picture of what's ahead as you can. But life in the academy, or life in the garret, is always a difficult life. The apprentice years are always difficult years when one wants to be more than one is.

GRAHAM: A significant percentage must drop out at midyear, don't they?

HARRISON: Right, many fail to take degrees. Many come not wanting simply to write, but wanting to teach. And we offer a degree program, and they have a job when they leave. There are lots of people, and you get them out of jail, and you befriend them, and you help them with broken axles on old automobiles, and life is life. I think you set up a climate, if possible, where creative writing is a part of the whole curriculum of the university, and where, beyond self-expression, good work is expected and high standards are set. And I think the younger students feel the infectiousness of this spirit around campus. It's been very exciting to watch it develop at Arkansas.

GRAHAM: I would suspect strongly that you do get a kind of *esprit de corps*—"It's us artists against the others."

HARRISON: That's right. When I first went to Arkansas, I don't think you'd have gotten fifty students together to see T. S. Eliot resurrected. But now it's different.

GEORGE GARRETT

Born 1929 in Orlando, Florida. Educated at Princeton University. Has taught at Wesleyan University, Rice University, the University of Virginia, Princeton, and Hollins College. At present is Professor of English at the University of South Carolina.

Books: (poetry) *The Reverend Ghost* (1957), *The Sleeping Gypsy* (1958), *Abraham's Knife* (1961), *For a Bitter Season: New and Selected Poems* (1967); (short stories) *King of the Mountain* (1958), *In the Briar Patch* (1961), *Cold Ground Was My Bed Last Night* (1964), *A Wreath for Garibaldi* (1969); (novels) *The Finished Man* (1959), *Which Ones Are the Enemy?* (1961), *Do, Lord, Remember Me* (1965), *Death of the Fox* (1971); (play) *Sir Slob and the Princess* (1962); (anthologies and texts) *New Writing From Virginia* (1963), *The Girl in the Black Raincoat* (1966), *Man and the Movies* (with W. R. Robinson, 1967), *New Writing in South Carolina* (with William Peden, 1971), *Film Scripts One* and *Film Scripts Two* (with O. B. Hardison, Jr. and Jane Gelfman, 1971), *The Sounder Few: Selected Essays from the Hollins Critic* (with R. H. W. Dillard and John Rees Moore, 1971), *Film Scripts Three* and *Film Scripts Four* (with O. B. Hardison, Jr. and Jane Gelfman, 1972).

THE WRITER'S VOICE

In the spring of 1973 William Morrow & Company will publish in both hardcover and softcover *The Writer's Voice: Conversations with Contemporary Writers*. Like *Craft So Hard To Learn*, it will consist of interviews conducted by John Graham at the Hollins Conference in Creative Writing and Cinema. Its editor is, again, George Garrett. However, *The Writer's Voice* is a much longer book than the present one and is not limited in its subject matter. The writers interviewed speak of their careers, their own work, and the work of other writers. These contributors are: R. V. Cassill, William Peden, Margaret Sayers Peden, Fred Chappell, Brian Moore, Richard Wilbur, Shelby Foote, Henry Taylor, Michael Mewshaw, William Manchester, James Seay, James Whitehead, Sylvia Wilkinson, Jonathan Baumbach, Ralph Ellison, James Dickey, David Slavitt, William Harrison, and R. H. W. Dillard.

The Writer's Voice is an important contribution to the small body of work in which writers, self-reflexive, ponder, aloud, their art.